VALUE INSTITUTE

LEAN
SIX
SIGMA

Guide For
Improving Healthcare

THE VALUE INSTITUTE
learning
center
AT DARTMOUTH-HITCHCOCK

Published by Mindstir Media, LLC
45 Lafayette Rd | Suite 181| North Hampton, NH 03862 | USA
1.800.767.0531 | www.mindstirmedia.com

Printed in the United States of America
ISBN-13: 978-1-7334732-8-6
Library of Congress Control Number: 2019913806

LEAN
SIX
SIGMA

Guide For
Improving Healthcare

DANIELLE M. POTTER, MS, LSSBB, PMP

NICOLE SZALAY BATULIS, MHA, LSSMBB, CPHQ

Table of Contents

Foreword

This book reflects the culmination of decades of work to build a state-of-the-art toolkit for process improvement in healthcare. Dartmouth-Hitchcock has a rich history of focusing on three core values: putting the needs of patients first, interdisciplinary team-based care, and a commitment to always learning and improving our care delivery systems. "Always learning and improving" characterizes our journey towards building a high-reliability organization that achieves the best outcomes possible for our patients. This journey included many methods, tools, experts, and examples of both success and failure to achieve our goals.

By 2010, Dartmouth-Hitchcock had experts and experience with the clinical microsystems approach, Baldridge, Studer, Toyota Lean, Six Sigma, Human Factors and the IHI collaborative improvement model. These pockets of expertise and lack of standardization led to limited central organizational support for local efforts, inconsistent results, and difficulty sustaining and/or spreading the improvements.

In my role as Chief Quality and Value Officer in 2011, I enlisted the help of a colleague and biomedical engineering professor, Dr. Susan McGrath, at Dartmouth College to help pull our experts together using a consensus and benchmarking process to establish the best methods, processes, and tools for improvement. We needed much broader, more consistent, efficient performance improvement to meet our strategic goal to be the highest quality and lowest cost provider for every service provided to our community. We have described the process used to identify best practices and develop the curriculum in detail in our article "Building a Foundation of Continuous Improvement in a Rapidly Changing Environment: The Dartmouth-Hitchcock Value Institute Experience" (McGrath & Blike, 2015)[1].

Learning, improving, and redesigning our care delivery systems remains THE critical capability of healthcare organizations to allow for our primary purpose, treating illness and restoring health, to be realized. The work of the Dartmouth-Atlas has helped the world understand that doing more tests and procedures and spending more money does not achieve better outcomes, nor a better experience. The methods and tools in this book have now been taught to all our staff at the basic level, over 3,000 staff at the intermediate level and to over 300 managers/leaders at the advanced-intermediate level. This book reflects the maturity of that experience and the many refinements from over eight years of use and improvement based on real-world experience. The "Dartmouth-Hitchcock DMAIC" tools, while anchored in Lean Six Sigma, comprise a flexible framework that is easy to understand. Furthermore, we have found this framework allows for additional tools to be added to the Define, Measure, Analyze, Improve, and Control buckets as we learn and grow.

But does it work? Our organizational improvement capacity and speed was limited mostly by our lack of discipline at the Define and Control phases of improvement initiatives early on. Over the last 8 years, our success in executing sustained improvement has been remarkable and unequivocally associated with driving improved outcomes. We have reduced our Serious Safety Events threefold, improved our overall safety rating on Consumer Reports to be the #1 of 17 teaching hospitals in New England, and reduced our cost

---

1 McGrath, S.P., & Blike, G.T. (2015). Building a Foundation of Continuous Improvement in a Rapidly Changing Environment: The Dartmouth-Hitchcock Value Institute Experience. *The Joint Commission Journal on Quality and Patient Safety*, 41(10), 435-444.

per discharge to be among the lowest for academic medical centers. Better outcomes at lower costs are achievable. Are we done? Of course not! However, I have confidence that our results are the product of the disciplined, data-driven, approach described in this book that is taught system-wide and used broadly to identify and execute improvements in our delivery system. I congratulate our team on this book, that reflects years of work and a multitude of contributions.

GEORGE T. BLIKE, MD, *Chief Quality and Value Officer at Dartmouth-Hitchcock Health*

As healthcare continues to face significant challenges, health systems and hospitals can only grow and cut so much. It is imperative that we work smarter and more efficiently. The tools and training offered by the Value Institute Learning Center are essential to helping Dartmouth-Hitchcock Health meet these challenges and ensure our financial sustainability and ability to care for the people in the communities we serve.

PATRICK F. JORDAN, III, MBA, *Chief Operating Officer at Dartmouth-Hitchcock Health*

Since its inception in 2011, the Value Institute programs have had a far-reaching impact on the quality of our care delivery. From reductions in our infection rates to improvements in operations and shared services, this training has touched all areas of our system. It continues to be a world-class program with demonstrated results.

SAMUEL N. SHIELDS, JR., MBA, LSSBB, CPHQ, *Vice President of Strategic Planning and Operational Excellence at Dartmouth-Hitchcock*

Introduction

Are you curious about how to apply Lean Six Sigma methodology to healthcare? Or maybe you are just one of those people who is constantly trying to make the work around you more efficient and easier to manage. Perhaps you heard about Lean in healthcare and this was the first book you found. Maybe you were told to start applying these improvement concepts to your work and you're reading this book against your will.

Regardless of your reasoning for picking it up, you have come to the right place. In this book we're going to give you the lowdown on all things Lean Six Sigma in healthcare. This book is written by Blackbelts who have been using Lean Six Sigma in healthcare for years. They are dedicated to improving their workplace, and they love teaching and getting others excited about doing improvement work. I know, they sound kind of nerdy, but I promise, these Blackbelts know their stuff and they're going to make sure that you have the knowledge necessary to execute a Lean Six Sigma project after reading this.

This book is designed to help healthcare clinicians and staff apply the Lean Six Sigma framework for completing a project that will help to improve quality, increase employee engagement, or reduce costs. We don't care what your title is! All that matters to us is that you want to improve your workplace. We have been teaching Lean

Six Sigma classes at our organization for many years and we teach everyone these skills: managers looking for techniques to improve their business units, clinical nurses looking to improve the quality of care delivered to their patients, secretaries who want to streamline some of their processes for managing patients, directors who want to help increase access to their clinics, providers who want to improve their clinic efficiency or reduce variation in practice, and support staff who want to improve the workflows within their areas to better service the needs of the departments they interact with. Lean Six Sigma is really applicable to anyone. You can utilize these skills at any level. All you need is a willingness from your leadership to let you try and a commitment to utilizing the process outlined in this book.

One thing this book is not designed to do is to take the place of formal training in Lean Six Sigma. Lean Six Sigma training is offered in many formats, typically at the following levels: Whitebelt, Yellowbelt, Greenbelt, and Blackbelt. I know you're confused – you're probably looking at the cover, perhaps reading the back of the book again…they said this was about healthcare improvement? Why are they talking about karate? We get that a lot. While the various types of training in Lean Six Sigma do follow a very similar format to training levels in martial arts, I can assure you that we are not qualified to give you any advice on karate training. Remember when I said we were kind of nerdy?

Whitebelt training is meant to give you a general awareness of Lean Six Sigma and the approach used, called DMAIC. DMAIC stands for Define, Measure, Analyze, Improve, and Control – you will learn more details about this later. You're going to get that knowledge and then some from reading this book. Yellowbelt training prepares people to lead small-scale improvement projects using the DMAIC framework or be active participants on a larger-scale project. Greenbelt training is typically designed for people who are going to lead improvement projects that are a little bit larger (we'll talk more about scoping a project in the next chapter) and a little bit more complex. And lastly, Blackbelt training prepares people to lead projects that cross multiple areas and include complex change management. As you can imagine, each level of training gets progressively more in depth. This book is designed to be supplemental to formal training – you don't need to have training before reading it, but if it sparks your interest, then you might consider heading in that direction. If you're already trained and this information is old hat, then use it as a reference. We have written it with a cover-to-cover flow, but you can jump right to the tool you need help on or a specific area to refresh your memory, if that is your preference. You'll probably miss some of our fantastic jokes, but we support your effort to be efficient in obtaining the information you need! In addition, the depth of knowledge that we cover is most consistent with typical Greenbelt training programs. If you're thinking you might execute at a Yellowbelt level, then you might not use all of this information, and that is totally fine! Use what works for you and your specific project. If you're operating at a Blackbelt level, then this is going to be a great reference guide but will not contain all of the advanced statistics and tools that you might need. We love those stats, sadly we *really* do, but we also want people to actually read this book, so we've designed it for the average Lean Six Sigma user.

When we get ready to dive into the process and the tools, we will introduce you to two DMAIC healthcare projects. These projects will help us to illustrate how the tools are applied to real work in healthcare. Both are based on project topics that we have tackled but have been fictionalized for the purpose of sharing. Read the project background information in the callout boxes to learn about both projects and better understand the examples provided throughout the book.

One last piece of need-to-know information before you start your journey with us: for all of the math-related concepts and tools, we will be using Microsoft Excel and an add-on package called SPC XL that allows for more advanced statistics than the traditional program. The photos that we will show of the outputs from our data analysis will be created using SPC XL. If you have another statistical program that you already use, your outputs might look a little different, but their interpretation will be the same. We will keep our description of how to summarize and manipulate data fairly general so as not to be too program specific, but we wanted you to be aware of our software choice.

Okay, enough about the book. You didn't buy this book so that you could learn about the structure of a book. You bought it so that you could learn about Lean Six Sigma and how it can be applied to healthcare. So, let's talk a little bit about that. You're going to hear us use words like continuous improvement, process improvement, and performance improvement. We will use them interchangeably because they all boil down to the same thing – being better tomorrow than you were today. Lean Six Sigma is a blended approach of two different methodologies that try to do just that. The first, Lean, is a concept that started decades ago at Toyota. Used in the manufacturing industry since then, it started to spread into healthcare in the early 2000s (Liker, 2004)[1]. The second, Six Sigma, is an approach pioneered at Motorola and then adopted across multiple industries in the years to follow (Breyfogle, 2003)[2]. Both are used widely in healthcare today, and if you're not using them already, then you certainly should be! While Lean focuses on removing waste from systems and creating value for customers, Six Sigma focuses on reducing variation and removing defects from processes. And if you work in healthcare, then I don't have to tell you how necessary these are right now!

Healthcare is expensive and the processes that we use to do our work are full of waste and redundancy. So much of what happens in a healthcare process doesn't add any value to the patient at all. How many people does a patient really want to talk to before getting a medication refilled? I'll give you my answer: zero! I just want the medication that I've taken for years without having to talk to a sec-

---

1 Liker, J. K. (2004). *The Toyota Way: 14 Management Principles From The World's Greatest Manufacturer*. McGraw Hill, New York.

2 Breyfogle, F. W. III. (2003). *Implementing Six Sigma: Smarter Solutions Using Statistics Methods, 2nd Ed.* John Wiley & Sons, Inc., New Jersey.

retary and a nurse and then wait for the nurse to call me back and then wait for the provider to call the pharmacy and then wait for the pharmacy to fill it. Now I'm not going to suggest that we don't have processes and protocols in place for a reason, as many of those reasons are valid. But what I am saying, is that our processes are also cumbersome for patients to navigate and the amount of time that our staff spend doing unnecessary tasks and our patients spend waiting is pretty high. But I probably don't need to tell you that, after all, it's why you bought the book! In addition to waste, we have so much variation in our processes that my mind can barely process it all! There is variation in the way that managers run clinics, variation in the way that nurses or providers practice medicine, and variation in how departments like finance and human resources carry out their work. All of this variation leads to unpredictable results and a lot of confusion for everyone. And do I really need to talk about defects in healthcare? We all know what those are. We know the severity of their consequences. When we carry out processes in healthcare it may not *always* be brain surgery, but it is always important for us to remember the consequences of not performing a process reliably.

So, there you have it, in one paragraph we have managed to convince you that both Lean and Six Sigma are needed in healthcare. I'm sure that a handful of people who read this are still feeling skeptical, and we get that. We can't convince everyone that this is the right methodology with words alone. Some people need to see it to believe it. So, I'm not going to ask you to believe us just because we wrote a book (after all, anyone can write a book), but I am going to ask you to keep an open mind. We didn't invent anything in this book. These are all tools and concepts that have been used for years. Read through the rest of it and give the process a try. If you don't see results, ask yourself if you really followed the process. If you give this an honest shot and have the leadership support needed to make meaningful change, you'll see the benefit for yourself.

Project Overviews

Both of our example projects focus on the surgical patient population in areas that were identified by leadership as key strategic focus areas. Surgical patients receive care in outpatient clinics, inpatient units, and the operating room/perioperative services.

PATHWAY TO DISCHARGE PROJECT

Our hospital has two 20-bed inpatient units for surgical patients. Each of these units has their own nursing staff. At project initiation, 8% of the patients on the surgical inpatient units (1 North and 3 North) were being discharged before 11:00 AM. The average discharge time of day was 2:40 PM. This was leading to backups in the perioperative services area, including the Post-Acute Care Unit (PACU), for patients waiting to be admitted to an inpatient surgical bed. Additionally, the broad set of stakeholders supporting the discharge process had expressed dissatisfaction with the coordination, communication, and timeliness of the current state workflow. The physician leader for The Department of Surgery sponsored a project to look at this flow and improve the discharge time of day for patients on these two units. The project team was made up of nursing staff, surgical residents, IT staff, physical therapy, and care management staff.

OPHTHALMOLOGY CLINIC FLOW PROJECT

The Ophthalmology clinic is made up of seven subspecialties. Each of these subspecialties has their own patient population that requires workup by a technician, a visit with the provider, and additional testing or imaging as required per the diagnosis. At project initiation, the average appointment cycle time in Ophthalmology was two hours. Patients were dissatisfied with their experience in clinic, providers and staff were dissatisfied with their day, and hospital leadership believed the long cycle times were preventing providers from seeing more patients. To keep the scope manageable, the physician leaders for the Departments of Surgery and Ophthalmology co-sponsored a project to work on improving flow and decreasing cycle time in the Retina subspecialty clinic. The project team included secretaries and technicians from both the Retina clinic and other subspecialties, as well as a Retina provider.

Chapter One:
Project Preparation

Before we dive into the details of the DMAIC process, we want to help you consider the prework that goes into a DMAIC project. There are a number of items to check off your to-do list before kicking off an improvement project. We've broken these down into five simple steps to consider before launching a project.

STEP 1: PICK A PROJECT

If you're like us, there is probably no shortage of projects that you could choose to tackle for your first Lean Six Sigma project. But it is important to make sure that you pick a project that is appropriate for the DMAIC framework. Let's talk through what a DMAIC project is and what it is not.

DMAIC is an acronym that stands for Define, Measure, Analyze, Improve, and Control. These are the five phases of a Lean Six Sigma project. DMAIC is a framework specifically used with problem-solving projects. People do projects in their daily work all the time, but not all of those projects are suited for a DMAIC approach. If someone is rolling out a new software, implementing a new training program, or adapting an evidence-based best practice; those are great projects, but they are not DMAIC projects. A DMAIC project is one that identifies a problem that has an unknown solution. For example, if patient wait times in clinic are high, we may need to do a project to reduce clinic wait times, but we may not know the best way to do that. This is where DMAIC helps us. By following the five project phases, we will come to better understand our problem, why it is happening, and determine the best course of action for resolution.

Sometimes we see problems that need to be fixed right away, and a DMAIC project might take too long. This is most common with corrective action plans. If an incident occurs and mitigation to prevent that from occurring again is needed immediately, then by all means, mitigate it now! Sometimes this is referred to as "containment", or a temporary fix until the process can be fully analyzed. Many of the problems that we have in healthcare such as long wait times and high costs lend themselves well to the DMAIC approach. Utilizing DMAIC helps to ensure that we are truly addressing the root causes of a problem rather than just treating the symptoms. If only symptoms are addressed, then there is risk of the problem reoccurring.

Ideally, projects are chosen in a somewhat organized fashion. We don't want to play whack-a-mole with problems in our work area and just keep going after them willy-nilly. Instead, projects should be aligned to the overall strategic objectives of an organization and prioritized accordingly. Lucky for you, we know clear strategic alignment isn't always reality and can give other prioritization tips as well. We've seen various levels of readiness for strategic alignment and just because it may not exist in your organization, does not mean that you can't do DMAIC projects. If you have strategic priorities at the organizational, or department level, then our suggestion is that you start there for identifying projects. Find out what work needs to be done and see if there is anything on the list that might lend itself to the DMAIC problem-solving process. Chances are there probably is.

If you know the organizational priorities that you can align department work to, consider drafting a strategy A3 as a way to keep goals and tactics organized in your area. If your area already has a strategy A3 or similar strategy documentation, review it for opportunities.

Tool: Strategy A3

PURPOSE: To document a plan that outlines goals, tactics, and measures for executing on the business plan for the fiscal year.

HOW TO COMPLETE:

1. Start by filling in general information at the top of the A3. Identify the business unit, the appropriate leaders, the fiscal year, and the focus area or pillars.

2. Next, identify the key organizational priorities that your department can help work on. These are typically areas where improvement opportunities exist. Indicate the current department performance, the goal, and the deviation from that goal. For example: an organizational priority might be improving patient satisfaction, the current department performance might be 70%, the goal is 90%, therefore the gap is 20%.

3. In the box next to the goals and performance, there is an opportunity to write notes about reasons for these performance gaps.

4. In the following section, "Tactics & Actions to Achieve Performance Goals", list the specific department initiatives that will address the gaps and help the department to meet the business goals for the fiscal year.

   a. The first column lists the tactic and the second column lists the "framework" of the tactic. Is this a project, a series of plan-do-study-act cycles, or something else?

b. The third column assigns ownership for this tactic, followed by the next two columns that indicate when the initiative will start and when it will be completed.

c. The sixth column is "Related Org. Priority" – this is where you would tie the tactic to the organizational priority that you identified in section two. Which of the priorities does this target specifically address?

d. In the seventh column, list the expected benefits, followed by the perceived barriers to this tactic. Rate the barrier risk (1 = low, 5 = high)

e. In the tenth column, list the resource score. This indicates the number of resources that will be needed (1 = I have the existing resources, 2 = I can build the skills on my team, 3 = I will need resources from somewhere else in the organization).

f. The current status column uses red, yellow, and green indicators to track the current status of the project in relation to milestones:

    i. Green: on track; Yellow: missed milestones but closure date on track; Red: missed milestones and closure date extended or at risk.

g. The last column is for indicating the benefit achieved thus far. This column is primarily used when updating the document and attending reviews with senior leaders.

5. The bottom of the document has two additional sections. The "Help and Resource Needs" section is the place to expand on any resource or barrier concerns. Outline the help necessary to support these tac-

tics. "Next Steps" is a section that will evolve as you progress through the fiscal year. If meeting quarterly or monthly with senior leaders, this box would likely change and need to be updated for each meeting.

Tips:

- Strategy A3 format, structure, and content can vary widely from organization to organization. The example displayed below has evolved over time at D-H (and may change too!)
- This is a document that should be used for both planning and revising work as the fiscal year progresses. This helps to outline those key tactics or actions that need to get done and should take priority over other work.
- Completing a strategy A3 requires a discussion between organizational leadership and local leadership to understand what is attainable.
- Benchmarking and an understanding of current state is essential in helping to set realistic performance targets and tactics.
- A strategy A3 is different than a problem A3 or a status A3, which you might have seen in other settings.

Example:
Surgical Services

Surgical Services completed a strategy A3 and outlined two projects as their focus for this fiscal year in the Our Patients strategic focus area.

BUSINESS UNIT	SURGICAL SERVICES		Focus	OUR PATIENTS
Clinical Lead	Sally Smith		**Fiscal Year**	
Admin Lead	Frank Johnson			

DEPARTMENT PERFORMANCE GOALS:				KNOWN REASONS FOR PERFORMANCE GAP:
Organizational Priority:	Current Performace	Performace Goal	Gap	
Improve Patient Access - Ontime OR Case Starts	80%	90%	10%	Outpatient surveys indicate that patients are unhappy with the length of their visit in clinic and the wait times at each visit. Additionally, patients and staff have expressed many frustrations with late inpatient discharges. More information is needed to determine reason for delay in discharge time.
Outpatient Experience - Overall Visit Rating	40%	85%	45%	
Reduce Capacity Denials- Increase Ontime Discharge	8%	40%	32%	

TACTICS & ACTIONS TO ACHIEVE PERFORMANCE GOALS:											
Tactic (A specific initiative aimed at achieving organizational priorities)	Tactic Framework (i.e. Project, Business Plan, PDSA, etc.)	Tactic Owner	Start Date	End Date	Related Org. Priority	Expected benefit	Perceived Barriers	Barrier Risk Score (1 being low risk, 5 being high risk)	Resource Score (1,2,3)	Current Status (red, yellow, green)	Benefit achieved thus far
Improve clinic flow in Ophthalmology	Lean Six Sigma Project	Sally/ Jim	7/5/19	12/20/19	Outpatient Experience	Increase patient satisfaction. opportunities to increase throughout	Current clinic layout and space configuration	3	2		
Improve ontime discharge rate on 1 North and 3 North inpatient units	Lean Six Sigma Project	Sally	1/5/19	6/30/19	Reduce Capacity Denials	Less bottlenecks in PACU. improved patient flow	Provider engagement	3	3		

HELP & RESOURCE NEEDS:	NEXT STEPS:
Will need representation from Care Management on the discharge work. Also anticipate provider champions will be needed for both clinic and discharge work, as provider practice change may be required. Will need to ensure that project leaders, Nancy Brown and Darcy Prince, are given time for Lean Six Sigma training and project work.	Enroll Nancy and Darcy in the Lean Six Sigma training program and contact Care Management to secure representation for the discharge work.

Projects can come from a variety of sources beyond strategic planning documents including, but not limited to:

- Staff noticing a problem in their daily work (quality or redundancy concerns).
- Results of patient experience surveys with suggested areas for improvement.
- Performance data that is not meeting the organizational or customer expectation.
- Benchmarking data that shows an opportunity for improvement.

These are some of the most common ways that people select a project to work on. Typically, there is a standard or an expectation and the current process is deviating from that standard. This might warrant a DMAIC project to better understand what is happening and assess possible solutions. For better chances of success try to keep these four things in mind when selecting a DMAIC project.

1. Choose a project that is close to your work and affects your role.
2. Pick something that you are passionate about improving (energy is contagious!).
3. Keep the scope of the project appropriate for your role. If you're involving other roles or departments, make sure they are invested in participating.
4. Choose a problem where the solution is not known.

When selecting a project you also want to be sure to think about the effort required to work on the project and how that compares to the potential impact a successfully completed project will have. Ideally, you want to focus on projects that will have a high impact. If you're looking at projects that will have low levels of impact, then make sure that the time invested in those projects is appropriate.

Some organizations may also be interested in the return on investment (ROI) associated with the project. Return on investment calculates the ratio between the expected profits of the project and the costs associated with investing resources into the project initiative. This can sometimes be difficult to quantify in dollars in healthcare when the improved outcomes are lower risk of harm, or greater patient satisfaction. If your organization already tracks the ROI of projects, then it can be a great way to help prioritize work by identifying those projects that will have the highest financial impact. Another way that your organization might prioritize projects is by looking at their net present value (NPV). NPV is another way to assess the anticipated financial benefit of a project (earnings) against the anticipated costs. Very similar to the ROI, you would be looking for a project with a higher NPV when prioritizing work.

STEP 2: PICK A SPONSOR

Choosing a sponsor for your project is one of the most important elements of setting your project up for success. ~~Some, few,~~ virtually zero projects run from start to finish without a hitch. It is common to reach out to the sponsor of the project for guidance or assistance along the way. A project sponsor is someone who has the proper authority to support the project team, keep the team apprised of information related to the project, and remove barriers to project success.

Here are some key things that a good sponsor should do:

- Have a high level of ownership over the process. If the process crosses departments or lines of authority, consider having co-sponsors so that all areas of the work are represented.
- Appreciate the importance of the work and believe that this project is a priority.
- Be available and accessible. Think about a tree falling in the woods: if you get a senior leader to support your project, but

he/she is never available for project updates or when you encounter a barrier, then do you really even have a sponsor? I don't know about the original riddle, but here the answer is "no".

- Publically support the project.
- Remove barriers to success. This is absolutely key. If you have a choice between sponsors because there are a few roles that make sense and one of those choices is particularly conflict averse, he/she might not be the best choice. You need a sponsor with the authority and the commitment to the project's success to slay any obstacles that get in your way. IT says they don't have time to make a change to the EMR? You need your sponsor to step up to the plate and slay that dragon! (Please be advised: the authors of this book are in no way endorsing the harm of IT staff; barrier removals typically only consist of civil conversations and moderate levels of influence.)
- Assist the project team as needed throughout and ensure accountability to a process owner (the person responsible for the process after the project) upon project completion. At the end of a project, the changes in practice and the ongoing monitoring of success needs to be incorporated into daily operations. We will talk more about this in the Control chapter. For now, when it comes to sponsor selection, you need assurance that the sponsor will make sure that you as the project leader don't end up doing work that is outside of your normal scope forever. He/she needs to help identify the correct operational leader to carry the torch once the project is done.

STEP 3: IDENTIFY A PROJECT TEAM

We have been referencing the idea of a project team for a little while now. Once you've identified your project topic and sponsor, the team is the next element that needs to be decided. Lean Six Sigma projects are not meant to be undertaken as solo endeavors, they are team efforts! With Lean Six Sigma, we believe that the people who best understand the problems and are best equipped to solve them are the people doing the work.

A project team should be made up of multiple perspectives and include representation from all areas of the work. Remember the scene in *Oceans 11* when they walk through the key players they need on their team? Or maybe you're more of a *The Fast and The Furious* type so you might recall when they do the same thing in *Fast Five*? Both of these scenes have one thing in common – they know the roles and types of people that they need on their teams, and they identify people who will specifically fulfill those needs. Now, you're not pulling together a group of criminals to pull off a heist (if you are, I think you might have purchased the wrong book), but you are pulling together a group of people to solve a problem. It is important that the team be made up of the right roles. If a large portion of your work involves nursing, but you don't have a nurse on the team, that's a problem.

Ensuring proper representation is important for two reasons:

1. In order to truly understand the problem and the current state of the process, you need to have front line staff sitting at the table. Assuming we know how people carry out their portion of the work is not going to cut it here. Every project that features a multidisciplinary team will shed light on what someone does that was previously unknown to the others.

2. Being part of the process, helps to ensure buy-in and commitment to project outcomes. Most of the time a Lean Six Sigma project results in a different process than the one that is currently being used. Staff can feel resistant to these changes if they don't feel like they've had any say in the solution. If you include them upfront, and take them on the journey of understanding the problem, they will likely understand the

solution and will hopefully support it and advocate for it with their peers.

Another thing to consider when building the team is the size. A typical project team includes between four and six people, not including the project leader. That seems to be the magic number, where there are enough perspectives without having so many perspectives that every meeting feels like participating on a hung jury. Some projects will end up with more or less, as it is critical to include roles that you think are important for project understanding and success. Just keep in mind that you don't need to have every secretary sitting at the table if their role in the process is limited; one should suffice. Alternatively, if you have a process that is made up predominantly of nursing work, perhaps you want to have two nurses on the team to provide a well-rounded perspective.

In some cases, it might not make sense to have a particular role at the table. A good example of this is a provider (physician, nurse practitioner, physician's assistant – or other care team member responsible for seeing patients). If you are working on a project to improve patient satisfaction with the scheduling process (but not adjusting provider scheduling templates), you probably don't need a provider as part of the core project team. Instead, you could have a provider who is your "ad-hoc" member. They are the provider who can give you information necessary for the project and help champion any changes in workflow, but they don't need to participate in every aspect of the conversation. Consider ad-hoc membership, not just for providers, but for anyone who the process touches only peripherally. It can be good to get participation and to keep staff informed, but if people are asked to be a part of project teams when they aren't really needed, it might inhibit their ability to be on project teams where they would be essential.

STEP 4: SCOPE THE PROJECT APPROPRIATELY

Ensuring that a project is properly scoped will help to increase the chances of project success. There are multiple adages that reflect this concept but the most well-known in the business world is probably: Don't try to boil the ocean! This phrase refers to taking on more than one can handle. When we think about project work, we want to make sure that the project is well-defined and includes guidelines for what will be addressed and what will not be addressed. This is really important, because remember how I said healthcare has a lot of problems? Well, it's our experience that when you pull back one layer of the onion, the others suddenly become clearer. So starting to uncover the reasons for one problem might lead to uncovering lots of other problems that are related but different. Without establishing boundaries for what is in scope and out of scope up front, it can be easy for the team or the sponsor to want to take on more than is reasonable with the one project.

Obviously what we're telling you is that you should only focus on the problem you are tasked with solving and ignore all of the other problems. Sweep them under the rug if you can. Wait, that doesn't sound right... If you find other problems you should absolutely make note of them. They could be things that could easily be addressed by someone outside the scope of the project or by another project team. Tell the sponsor and/or the appropriate operational leader. Do not sweep them under the rug. I repeat, do not sweep them under the rug! But just as important as it is to stress that the whole rug thing was a joke, it is important to stress that you should not add these additional problems to the scope of your project. It may seem simple, innocent, easy, even helpful at first. But soon, you will experience the dark side, what project leaders refer to as scope creep. Dun, dun, dun.

Scope creep is the kryptonite of project work. In small doses it might cause minor setbacks, or barely noticeable distress, but in large doses it can completely cripple your ability to move forward. Scope creep is when you bend the scope of your project a little bit to fix another problem, or to add another component of work. Typically, this is done in small, iterative steps. Sometimes you may not even realize it is happening until your scope has creeped too much. A successful project is set up with the scope appropriate for the project team and the issue being tackled. Then, it is the responsibility of the sponsor, the project leader, and the project team to ensure that scope creep does not occur.

In some instances, the scope of the project may need to be adjusted as you learn more about the problem. While this typically means narrowing a scope, occasionally a scope can widen if the team determines that it is necessary in order to address the problem. Never change the scope of a project without first talking to the sponsor.

Use the graphic below to help understand the relationship between scope, impact, and Lean Six Sigma training levels. The scope of a project should always be discussed upfront with the sponsor.

STEP 5: DETERMINE PROJECT STRUCTURE

The last thing to consider when launching a project are the logistics for how the project will be conducted. This primarily refers to the length and frequency of meetings. How often is your team going to meet to work on this project? What is the timeline allotted for the project? How will meetings be conducted?

Some of this might seem unnecessary to consider, especially so early on. Do I really need to think about meeting frequency and length upfront? We are all adults - won't we just schedule and show up to meetings as we go? But we're here to say – yes, you do need to think about these things! A proper project plan is very important for project success. Without one, we have seen many a project go on and on and on....practically all the way to infinity and beyond.

Components of Project Structure:

1. **Timeline**: Establish the timeline for the project. When do you need to finish the project? Are there any outside reasons for a specific deadline such as regulations or departmental goals? If you do not have a hard deadline, think about what is reasonable for the problem that you're trying to solve. We typically recommend about a month for each phase of DMAIC – know that data collection and piloting of solutions will likely be the longest sections of your project and could take anywhere from two to six weeks each.

2. **Meeting length and frequency**: Based on the overall timeline, think about the cadence of your meetings. The shorter the timeline, the more often the team should probably meet. People typically fall into one of two patterns: weekly meetings or biweekly meetings. A strong argument could be made for the benefits of each, so this really depends on what works best for the team members. Weekly meetings are great to keep people on track and can occasionally be cancelled when a team meeting is not necessary on a given week. If

meeting weekly, 60 minute meetings are usually sufficient. Biweekly meetings are often preferred by busy leaders. While they can be equally as effective, there are a couple of things to consider. First, consider making the meeting longer. Since you are meeting less often, try to meet for 90 minutes to get more accomplished. Also keep in mind that more work outside of meetings might be required. This is part of the give and take with meeting less often – ensure that team members know that completing assignments between meetings will be required regardless of cadence but more may be required when having biweekly meetings.

3. **Meeting roles**: Finally, think about how you want to conduct meetings. You should consider having established roles for each meeting. There should be a timekeeper, a scribe, and a leader. Usually as the project leader, you will be leading most meetings. Ask team members to take notes or assist with activities on the whiteboard. One team member should be assigned to keep track of time for the meetings. We will share tips as we go for tools that might benefit from these roles.

To assist you with the organization of the meeting, you should regularly utilize two tools: a meeting agenda and meeting minutes. The template or structure for these is not as important as actually having them. Many organizations have a version of their own and you should feel free to utilize those. We have included examples of the templates that we use for your reference.

Meetings without agendas can quickly go awry with too much time given to one item. Even worse, without proper planning and thinking through of the agenda, meetings are led without clear meeting objectives and outputs. Forcing yourself to create an agenda (which is usually super quick to do!), forces you to spend a few minutes thinking about the meeting upfront so that you know what outputs are required at the end of the meeting. No one wants to attend another meeting with an aimless objective – we already do enough of that – so make sure you are prepared and respecting the time of your team members.

Tool: Meeting Agenda

PURPOSE: To prepare for an upcoming meeting and share the outputs and agenda items with the team in advance of the meeting.

Example:
Ophthalmology Clinic Flow Project

Review the agenda for the Ophthalmology Clinic Flow Project kickoff meeting.

MEETING AGENDA

Project Name: Ophthalmology Clinic Flow
Date: 7/10
Time: 1:00-2:00PM
Location: Main Conference Room

Meeting Leader: Nancy Brown
Recorder/Timekeeper: Joe Smith

Participants: Nancy Brown, Joe Smith, Sally Smith, Erika Thompson, Jeff Larson, Jill Chapman

Objective/Outputs: Completed project charter

Agenda Item	Presenter(s)	Time Allotted	Notes
Team Introductions	Nancy	10 minutes	
Ice Breaker Activity	Nancy	15 minutes	
Review of Project Charter	Nancy/Team	25 minutes	
Next Steps	Nancy	10 minutes	

Next meeting: 7/21 at 1:00PM, Main Conference Room

Tool: Meeting Minutes

PURPOSE: To document the discussions and actions in a meeting to ensure that all team members have a reference for the meeting and all action items are documented.

Example:
Ophthalmology Clinic Flow Project

MEETING MINUTES

Project Name: Ophthalmology Clinic Flow
Date: 7/10

Participants: Nancy Brown, Joe Smith, Sally Smith, Erika Thompson, Jeff Larson, Jill Chapman

Not Available: None

Agenda Item	Discussion
Team Introductions	Nancy explained that we were all selected to work on the Ophthalmology clinic flow project. Nancy is the clinic operations manager, Joe is the lead physician, Sally is the technician manager, Erika is a technician, Jeff is the administrative supervisor, and Jill is a secretary.
Ice Breaker Activity	We did an ice breaker activity with skittles and answered questions about ourselves based on the color of three skittles that we each had.
Review of Project	Nancy had drafted a project charter that set up the basis for the clinic flow project. We talked through the problem statement, business case, scope, and the project goals. We also agreed to 90-minute biweekly meetings in order to hit the organizational deadline of 12/20. See the attached charter document for full details.
Next Steps	For the next meeting we will be working on a SIPOC. Team members should review this tool from the training and be prepared to talk about the flow steps in their areas.

Action Item	Responsible Person	Date Due
SIPOC Review	All team members	7/21

Best practice is to send a meeting agenda at least two days in advance of the meeting and to send out the meeting minutes within two days of the meeting. Note that depending on your meeting frequency, these times can be adjusted to meet team communication needs. This helps all team members to stay apprised of what is occurring at meetings and helps to ensure staff follow-up on any action items. Be as consistent as possible in this to help keep the team and the project on track.

Once you have thought about the five steps in this chapter, you are ready to kick-off your project! Often, the first meeting is called a "kick-off meeting" and should be used to generate some excitement over working on this problem together. An agenda for a kick-off meeting typically includes team introductions and some sort of ice breaker activity (there are thousands of these available on the internet, select one that will work well for your group!). We recommend doing ice breakers even if you already know each other, because this can be a great way to learn about each other and connect in a different way. Following that, if the sponsor can attend the meeting to show support and help explain why the project is a priority, that is recommended. Staff will put more stock in a project when it is clear that a leader is making this a priority and is supportive of the team's work. Lastly, use the rest of the meeting to review or draft a charter to start to understand project specifics, and then determine your meeting structure going forward.

Now, let's kick-off the core of this book and talk about the first phase of a DMAIC project, Define.

Chapter Two:
Define

The first phase of a DMAIC project starts with Define. In order to truly solve a problem, we have to understand what the problem is and that starts with properly defining it. During the Define phase you will focus on three primary goals: initiating the project, identifying stakeholders, and capturing customer feedback about the problem. Let's look at each of these three areas in detail and talk about some of the tools that can support these objectives.

PROJECT INITIATION

A lot of the work of project initiation really happens upfront. You have actually started the Define phase from the moment that you identify the project and start to think through the steps that we covered in Project Preparation. Since we already covered sponsor selection and team member selection in detail, we won't talk about that again now. If you are reading this out of order, then you have two choose-your-own-adventure style options: flip back to chapter one and figure out what the heck it is we are talking about or continue reading and hope it all starts to make sense eventually.

Assuming you did the prework for setting up the project that we recommended (because by now you have discovered that following your Jedi master's advice is wise), your first step in Define is really to create your project charter.

The project charter is a document that provides an outline of the problem, the scope, the goals or objectives, and the business case for why this problem should be addressed. The charter also serves as a contract between the sponsor and the project team, giving the team the authority to address this problem and providing them with a commitment of support from the sponsor.

Sometimes sitting down with a blank charter can feel overwhelming. You might wonder where to start or what pieces of information are the most important to include. To assist you, we have created a charter development worksheet that will break down components of the charter into simple questions. When you start to combine your answers to these questions, you'll have a pretty good first draft of your charter to share with your sponsor and project team. Check out the example in the callout boxes to show how the charter development worksheet helped to support the creation of the project charter for the Pathway to Discharge project.

Also, as you draft the charter, keep in mind that the charter will evolve throughout the course of the project. You may not have all of the data that you'd like up front, but you can go back and add this information as it becomes available. You can also amend the goals as you get additional information about the current state.

Tool: Charter Development Worksheet

PURPOSE: The charter development worksheet asks specific questions directed at various elements of the charter. The completed worksheet should feed directly into a complete problem statement, business case, and project scope for the project charter.

HOW TO COMPLETE:

1. Step one is designed to identify the project scope. This can be broken down by identifying the start and stop points of the process being looked at and by clearly defining what that process is.

2. Step two focuses on the problem statement. Creating the problem statement is broken down into thinking about four separate elements. When combined, the answers to these questions will help formulate a concise and specific problem statement.

   a. What is happening today and how is this different from the goal?

   b. Who is currently impacted by this problem?

   c. When in the process does the problem occur?

   d. Where is this problem happening?

3. The third and final step is to focus on the business case. Again, it can be nice to break down the business case into five different elements that when combined, create the final business case for the charter.

   a. How will the reduction of defects (or other indicated improvement) impact the customers?

   b. How will the reduction of defects (or other indicated improvement) impact the business?

   c. How will the reduction of defects (or other indicated improvement) impact the employees?

   d. Why is it important to work on this now?

   e. What will happen if the process is not improved?

Tips:

- Try to think about the answer to each question independently. This can prevent being bogged down by coming up with the full problem statement or business case at once. The answers to these individual questions will help create specific and targeted statements for the charter.

Example:
Pathway to Discharge

STEP 1:   Define the process, where it starts and where it ends

The process **starts** with:	The process **is**:	The process **ends** with:
Discharge planning initiated for a surgical patient	Discharging a patient from the surgical inpatient nursing unit	Patient departs the surgical inpatient nursing unit

STEP 2:   Draft the project description/project purpose

What	Who	When	Where
Describe **what** is happening today and the difference between current performance and goal	Identify **who** is impacted by the problem	Specify **when** in the process the problem occurs	Indicate the location for the problem
Currently only 8% of patients are discharged before 11:00AM and average discharge time is 2:40PM. We would like to target 1:00PM to support surgical patient flow	Surgical patients waiting for inpatient beds, providers interested in progressing their patient's care, and nursing unit staff	In the discharge planning process	Nursing units 1 North and 3 North

STEP 3:   Create the business case

Our Customers	Our Business	Our Employees	Why now?	What if?
How will the reduction of defects impact our customers?	How will the reduction of defects impact our business?	How will the reduction of defects impact our employees?	What makes it important to work on this problem now?	What will happen if we don't improve this process?
Patients will be discharged earlier and new surgical admissions will more easily access inpatient beds	Will increase the ability to handle growth in surgical case volumes and promote surgical patient flow	It will increase the staff's ability to support patients at the appropriate level of care	Increasing surgical case demand with limited space for inpatient bed expansion	Referral of surgical cases to outside facilities because we can not accommodate

Tool: Charter

PURPOSE: The charter provides a preliminary outline of the current problem, the project's scope and objectives, and identifies the participants in a project. It is a document that serves as a contract between the project sponsor and the project lead to transfer the project responsibility from the leadership team and sponsor to the project team. The charter is an evolving document that will continue to change over the course of the project. The charter is used to clarify expectations for the team, keep the team focused and aligned with organizational priorities, and estimate the project's potential impact on the business.

HOW TO COMPLETE:

1. Start by identifying a concise problem statement. This statement should explain what is happening today and identify the reason that the project is needed. Keep this statement as fact-based as possible. Use data and metrics related to the process to help substantiate the problem statement. (Reference your work from the charter development worksheet, if used.)

2. Next, complete the business case. This should explain why the project is important to others. Link the project to any relevant strategy or operational plans. If data is available use financial, quality, or safety baseline metrics or best practices to help explain current state. (Reference your work from the charter development worksheet, if used.)

3. Identify the scope of the project by describing what will be included and excluded in the project. This creates boundaries for the team's work and can help to prevent scope creep if the team tries to tackle more than they were originally charged with. Identify the scope by considering what types of things will be covered and what will not (i.e. insurance reimbursement) and also by defining the start and end of the process being addressed.

4. Next, think about goals and metrics. When thinking about goals, determine what the project will accomplish and what the expected benefit of the project will be. Goals should be SMART goals (specific, measurable, attainable, relevant, and time-bound). The metrics should be a standard for measuring or evaluating something. These metrics will be used to collect baseline data at the start of the project and to monitor improvement during the Control phase. Metrics will be used to determine if the project achieved its goals.

5. Milestones should be determined to outline how long the project will take. Typically, each phase of a DMAIC project is considered a milestone and assigning dates to each phase can help keep a project on track.

6. Finally, fill out the resource plan. This is where it is determined who will be the sponsor, leader, and team members for the project. Think about key stakeholders in the process when determining team members and make sure that they are adequately represented.

Tips:

- Remember that the problem statement and business case should be short and concise. Be as specific and data-driven as possible to ensure clarity and conciseness.

- When thinking about goals and metrics, make sure to think about measurable outcomes. For example, a goal to "get a better process" would not be a good goal as it is not specific or measurable.

- When thinking about project scope, think about what is in scope and also what is out of scope. It can be helpful to clearly state things that will not be addressed. This can be something like "the process after the patient is scheduled" or "changes to the medical record system", or whatever is deemed by the project team and the sponsor as something that the project team will not be tackling. Revisit scope throughout the course of the project and make sure that the team is still on track.

- Be realistic about setting milestone dates. Keep in mind things like holidays and summer vacations that can severely impact how fast the project work will move forward.

- Revisit the charter after completing the SIPOC (you will learn about this tool soon!) The SIPOC might identify other stakeholders that hadn't been considered and the team may wish to add some of them as team members before moving too far forward with the project.

Example:
Pathway to Discharge

The Pathway to Discharge team created a charter to start their project. Although the organizational goal was to discharge patients by 11AM, the team set a more attainable goal of improving the average discharge time of day to 1PM during the project.

PROBLEM STATEMENT
Currently very few patients are discharged before 11AM on the inpatient post-surgical units, 1N and 3N. Last year, 7.42% of patients on 1N and 6.23% of patients on 3N were discharged before 11AM. Discharges spike in mid-afternoon, between 2 and 3PM. This spike in discharges delays access to inpatient beds for new surgical admits and creates work overload for nurses and ancillary resources. There is an opportunity to better understand provider, nurse, patient, and ancillary department workflows for discharge planning, identify opportunities to better match the supply of inpatient beds with demand, and streamline workflows.

BUSINESS CASE
Delays in discharge on the inpatient surgical units can lead to downstream delays in moving patients out of the PACU, Main OR, Emergency Room, or a higher level of care. Any time patients spend in a medically unnecessary level of care costs the hospital money and delays patient placement. Additionally, delays in the OR can impact the number of cases completed in a day and patient, provider, and staff satisfaction.

PROJECT SCOPE	
In Scope: 1N & 3N surgical inpatient units	**Scope Exclusions:** 2N & 4N surgical inpatient units

GOAL	METRIC
Decrease average discharge time of day to 1:00PM	Average discharge time of day
100% completion of "estimated date of discharge" field in EMR	% of patients with intended/planned discharge data documented in advance of day of discharge
Improve patient satisfaction with the discharged experience on 1N & 3N	% patient satisfaction with discharge process (survey)
Rate the day, stakeholder rating of discharge process	Survey pre and post intervention

RESOURCE PLAN	
Project Lead(s):	Nursing Supervisor, Surgical Resident
Project Sponsor(s):	Surgical Department Chair & Surgical Unit Medical Director

TEAM MEMBERS	
1N Nurse 3N Nurse Urology NP	Oncology PA Physical Therapist
Social Worker Care Manager Patient Volunteer	EMR Specialist Pt. Placement Supervisor
Coaches: Physician Coach and Blackbelt Coach	

MILESTONES	
Define Tollgate	2/1
Measure Tollgate	3/1
Analyze Tollgate	4/1
Improve Tollgate	5/1
Control Tollgate	6/14

Once you have drafted your charter and reviewed it with both your sponsor and your team, you will be ready to start to identify your stakeholders. But before you do that, it can be helpful at this point in your project to draft an elevator speech. This is a very quick (60-120 second) speech about what your project is and what you hope it will accomplish. Having this prepared allows you, as the leader, and your team members to share a consistent message when talking about the project work.

Writing an elevator speech at this stage should be pretty easy, because you already have all of the information that you need to communicate on your drafted charter. Simply take the most important information from your problem statement and goals and consolidate it into just a few sentences about your project. The idea is that if you bumped into someone on an elevator, you would have enough time to give them a brief project update during the ride – so you can't have a speech so long that it would require you being on an elevator in the Empire State Building to get through it. Just like the charter, the elevator speech should be updated as the project progresses and more information is learned.

Tool: Elevator Speech

PURPOSE: An elevator speech is designed to communicate the essential elements of a project's vision and the need for change in a 60-120 second speech. The title comes from the idea that the speech is short enough to be delivered in the length of time it takes to ride an elevator.

HOW TO COMPLETE:

1. Think about the following elements and combine into a speech that can be delivered in 60-120 seconds:

    a. The current need for change

    b. Goals of the project

    c. Project progress (if applicable)

    d. What this means to you personally

    e. What this means to the organization

2. Practice on a colleague and revise as needed.

Tips:

- The elevator speech is something that will evolve over the course of the project. As the project progresses, it might be good to highlight some of the benefits already seen.

- Do not include a solution.

- Keep it concise.

- Do not over promise on a goal.

- Do not use language or acronyms that the audience might not be familiar with.

- The elevator speech should be adjusted based on the intended audience. Tailor the speech differently when trying to engage someone in the project or when asking someone for something. Sometimes a hook at the end can help with a difficult ask.

Example:
Pathway to Discharge

Right now, close to 50% of our patients are discharged between 1:00 PM and 4:00 PM in the afternoon on the surgical nursing units. This increases demand for work mid-afternoon for both nurses and housekeeping to turn over the beds. What we are trying to understand is the actual need for the beds during the day and determine if we can match the freeing-up of those beds – the discharge process - to demand from perioperative services so that our patients and clinical care team experience a much smoother flow. Our goal is to move the average discharge time of day from 2:40 PM to 1:00 PM. We recognize it's easy to point fingers at stakeholders and departments in a complex workflow like patient discharge -- but we believe the problem is complex and we need all stakeholders together to try and figure out what is causing the current state and how we can redesign it to make flow for patients throughout the organization better.

IDENTIFY STAKEHOLDERS

Stakeholders of a process are people who are impacted by the process. We need to identify these individuals and groups of people upfront, include some of them on the project team, and communicate regularly with them throughout the course of the project. In healthcare we have lots of stakeholders because we have a lot of people involved in our processes. While the ultimate customer in healthcare is the patient, we should remember that staff in all areas of the hospital are often stakeholders and customers of processes.

Identifying our stakeholders is important because we all know what it's like to be on the receiving end of a well-meaning initiative where we were notified only at the last minute. Without any understanding of how the decision-makers got to the decision and any clear understanding of how this change will impact us, we often feel defensive or resistant. We want to make sure you set up your project for success and that means making sure that some stakeholders are part of the change and decision-making, while the others are all at least kept aware of the project's progress as you go along.

A SIPOC is a great tool to help do this. The SIPOC stands for suppliers, inputs, process, outputs, and customers. The SIPOC has you breakdown the process into five to seven high-level process steps and identify the suppliers and inputs that go into each step, then the outputs and customers that come out of it. By doing this for the whole process, you end up with a list of suppliers and customers, which together make up your stakeholder group.

A supplier is someone who provides something for the given process step. The inputs are typically nouns that go into the process step. Outputs are things that come out of the step (this could be a noun or a state of being). Customers receive something as a result of this step.

Most likely when you complete a SIPOC, you will find that many of the stakeholders have representation on your team – which is great! When you selected your team members, you did so by identifying those groups of people who are impacted by the process. You did an initial review of project stakeholders at that time. But doing the SIPOC often reveals additional stakeholders, some of which may not have been considered before. This is important because it will help identify people that you should communicate with, sometimes people that you want to add to your team, and often customers that you should be talking to in the next step.

Tool: SIPOC

PURPOSE: A SIPOC stands for suppliers, inputs, process, outputs, and customers. The SIPOC is a high-level process map that helps team members to identify stakeholders by looking at the suppliers and customers of each process step. After completing a SIPOC, some teams might decide to include additional stakeholders on a project team.

HOW TO COMPLETE:

1. Name the process that is being documented.
2. Identify the beginning and end points of the process.
3. Fill in the remaining process steps (down the center of the SIPOC).
4. Fill in the suppliers, inputs, outputs, and customers of each process step.

Tips:

- There are a couple of ways to complete the SIPOC. Once the team has identified the process steps, the SIPOC can be worked linearly (start with the supplier of the first process step and work left to right) or vertically, identifying all outputs and customers, followed by all suppliers and inputs.

- It is very common for the outputs and customers of one process step to be the suppliers and/or inputs of the next process step.

- Keep in mind that an input or output could be a state, not just an object. For example, "roomed patient" or "updated patient chart" could be outputs of a process step.

- Remember to focus on current state not an ideal or future state.

- Keep the process high level with no more than 5-7 process steps. Also, keep the team from getting lost in the details and one-off situations. Try to think about the process as it happens 80% of the time.

- Suppliers and customers are people; inputs and outputs are things or states of being.

Example:
Pathway to Discharge

Below is the SIPOC created by the Pathway to Discharge team. The team used several abbreviations that we have defined for your reference. The team made a decision at the start of this activity to use fewer steps to list the process, but this meant that they were complex and included a lot of suppliers, inputs, outputs, and customers. Your team may choose to have more steps but have each step be less complex.

SUPPLIER	INPUT	PROCESS	OUTPUT	CUSTOMER
Patient, Attending, Resident	Admission Orders	**Decision to Admit**	Admitted Patient	Patient, Attending, Resident, Associate Provider, Clinical Nurse, Pharmacist, Ancillary Staff, Care Manager, LNA, PT/OT
Patient, Attending, Resident, Associate Provider, Clinical Nurse, Pharmacist, Ancillary Staff, Care Manager, LNA, PT/OT	Assessments	**Plan of Care Initiated and Carried Out**	Documentation in EMR, Care Team Discussion, Orders and Consults	Patient, Attending, Resident, Associate Provider, Clinical Nurse, Pharmacist, Ancillary Staff, Care Manager, LNA, PT/OT
Patient, Attending, Resident	Assessments, Lab/Test Results, Treatment Outcomes, Patient/Family Preferences	**Discharge Planning**	Discharge Orders, Transportation Plan, Disposition Plan (SNF, etc.), DME/Supply Plan, Patient/Family Teaching, Follow-Up Appointments, Radiology Orders, Prescriptions, Lab Orders	Patient, Attending, Resident, Patient's Family, Unit Secretary, Associate Provider, Clinical Nurse, Care Manager, LNA, PT/OT, Pharmacist, Ancillary Staff, Medical Supply Co., Transportation Provider, External Pharmacy, OP Schduler, Labs, Radiology, External Faciliaty/Agency, PCP/Referring Provider
Patient, Attending, Resident, Patient's Family, Unit Secretary, Associate Provider, Clinical Nurse, Care Manager, LNA, PT/OT, Pharmacist, Ancillary Staff, Medical Supply Co., Transportation Provider, OP Schduler, Labs, Radiology, External Faciliaty/Agency, PCP/Refer-ring Provider	Discharge Orders, Transportation Plan, Disposition Plan (SNF, etc.), DME/Supply Plan, Patient/Family Teaching, Follow-Up Appointments, Radiology Orders, Prescriptions, Lab Orders	**Patient Discharged**	Discharged Patient, Handoff Discussions, Follow-Up Documen-tation, Medications Picked Up, EVS Room Clean	Patient, Patient's Family, EVS, External Faciliaty/Agency, PCP/Referring Provider, Medical Sup-ply Co., Transportation Provider, External Pharmacy

LNA – licensed nursing assistant
PT/OT – physical therapy/occupational therapy
OP – outpatient
SNF – skilled nursing facility
EVS – environmental services
PCP – primary care provider
DME - durable medical equipment

CAPTURE CUSTOMER FEEDBACK

Once you have completed your SIPOC and gotten information about who your stakeholders are, it is important to get input from the customers of your process. In Lean Six Sigma, this process is called voice of the customer, and is the final step in the Define phase.

Voice of the customer is simply a term used for the process of understanding what it is that customers want from your product or service. In healthcare, we typically think about the healthcare services that a patient receives. However, there can be many different customers throughout the hospital who also receive a service from your process. A billing department handling insurance prior authorization requests is not only providing a service to the patient, but also to the department where that patient has an upcoming procedure. Both the department and the patient will be affected if the process does not deliver what they need – if not done properly, this could result in a cancelled appointment. The patient may experience a delay in care and the department may lose revenue if they are unable to backfill the procedure slot. In this case, you would want to gather the voice of the patient and the clinical departments being served.

The voice of the customer process can be broken down into three components:

- Capture stakeholder feedback
- Categorize feedback
- Translate feedback into measurable characteristics

Capture stakeholder feedback

The first component, capture stakeholder feedback, requires some thought about whose feedback will be captured and what the method for obtaining the feedback will be.

The voice of the customer (VOC) information can be obtained passively or actively. Passive would simply be taking in unsolicited feedback from your customers. If you receive frequent unsolicited complaints about something, then you are receiving the voice of your customer. The problem with unsolicited feedback is that it tends to come from customers who are on one of two ends of the spectrum – they were either very happy with your service and want to share that experience with you, or they were very dissatisfied and they want to tell you so that you can do better next time. Rarely will people give unsolicited feedback if they had a fairly neutral experience. To ensure that you obtain the voice of all customers, it is best practice to collect this information actively. Some of the most common ways to actively gather VOC are through surveys, 1x1 interviews, discussions at staff meetings, or focus groups. Regardless of the method used, you want to try to make sure that you are a getting a representative sample of responses. This should include satisfied customers, dissatisfied customers, and neutral customers. Depending on the service or process that you are evaluating, you may even want to include non-customers. Non-customers are people who choose not to go to your facility and receive a service somewhere else. Talking to them can help you understand what you are currently failing to provide or what someone else is providing better.

Surveys are a very common tool for collecting VOC responses because they are relatively easy and cheap to administer. There are free online survey creation sites that will send anonymous surveys, as well as low-tech options such as using a basic Microsoft Word document. Surveys are very useful because they can mix qualitative and quantitative responses. Qualitative responses are the open-ended questions that lead to specific comments. These are the most useful types of questions to ask and frequently yield the best VOC responses. In fact, if you want to truly gather VOC data, you cannot do it without asking open-ended questions. Without these, you won't have the substantive responses that are required. There is typically a tendency to want to ask customers about their satisfaction with the process during the VOC survey. While this is not a bad thing, remember that this is also not the primary focus of the survey. The goal is to get comments from customers that can be used to help identify the characteristics of your service that are most important to them. Inserting a question about overall satisfaction, using a Likert Scale, can be a great way to get a measurable baseline for customer satisfaction, but this should not be the only question format used. Overall satisfaction is a question that could also be asked after improvements to a process are made to determine if there has been a measurable change from the customer's perspective. Multiple choice questions can also sometimes be helpful when gathering information, but should be used in combination with comments and open-ended questions as well.

While there is an entire science devoted to minimizing biases in survey responses, a small VOC survey can usually be optimized by remembering a few key points.

- Be specific and use clear language. Do not leave questions up for interpretation or you may receive very different responses depending on how someone reads the question. Using specific language will help keep people on the topic that you intend for them to focus on. Without a clear question, patients might start sharing thoughts they have on various topics of frustration.

- Avoid leading questions. Asking a question such as "How frustrated are you with our scheduling process?" or "Were you frustrated by your last scheduling experience?" may seem like a good question at first, but you are subtly implanting a feeling onto the customer experience. Not only might this guide the customer's response, but it also limits thinking to frustrated or not frustrated. Instead, if you ask "How did you feel about your last scheduling experience?" you leave the door open for a multitude of responses. People can respond with frustration levels or other thoughts/feelings that they had.

- Keep it short. Asking people to fill out long surveys is a good way to end up with very short answers. Whether you're surveying patients or staff, people often don't have the time to spend on long surveys. A good rule of thumb is a maximum of ten questions, but less is almost always better, especially when surveying patients.

Even if you follow all of these tips, keep in mind that surveys will have a response bias. People get to choose whether or not they fill out a survey. Seriously, how many surveys do you fill out? The people most likely to want to respond are those that are really happy or really unhappy (or people like us authors who believe that every survey is used to make a positive change and thus get excited about filling them out – we at least recognize that we might be a bit unique). Do the best you can to try and solicit feedback from those in the middle. For staff, offer a small incentive for participating (free coffee or a raffle drawing) or send reminders to help trigger their responses.

Focus groups are also a great way to gather customer feedback. Focus groups are typically small group sessions with 5-10 participants, led by an unbiased third-party. While good information can be gathered in a focus group, they are generally more time-consuming and expensive than administering a survey. Focus groups require more of a resource requirement (space, leader, sometimes snacks, etc.), and can also present certain biases. One bias might be groupthink (originally developed by Irving Janis). This is when a group leans towards preferring harmony over having an honest, possibly dynamic, conversation. People will tend to agree without sharing the opinions that they think others might disagree with. Similarly, there is also a tendency for people to say what they think the facilitator wants to hear. This is why it is really important to have a third-party person leading the group, someone who the participants will view as impartial. Focus groups differ from a survey in that there may be prescribed questions to ask, but the facilitator can also use comments as a jumping-off point to dig deeper at his/her discretion.

Another option for collecting VOC responses is to conduct a one-on-one interview with customers in person or via the phone. This can leverage some of the benefits of each of the other methods, but also has some of the same drawbacks. While interpretation of questions might be less of an issue in-person, there might be a tendency for people to withhold honest responses if they perceive them as less favorable. When working with patients, many groups will choose to have a patient volunteer conduct these interviews, as patients might feel more comfortable giving honest responses to someone who does not work in the area where they are receiving care. These can also be time-consuming, so be sure to think about how many customers you will want to get responses from when deciding which method to use.

As you think through your customers and the methods for collecting their feedback, one tool that can help the improvement team think through the optimal way to collect responses is a voice of the customer plan. This is the first of many plans that we'll introduce you to – we pretty much have a plan template for everything, because we want you to think proactively about your project work.

If you're having trouble getting started, check out these sample questions to get you started:

- What do you like about this process? In what way have we met your expectations?
- In what way have we not met your expectations? What could we do differently?
- What are some suggestions you have for improving our service?
- What is most important to you when receiving care with us?

Tool: Voice of the Customer Plan

PURPOSE: The voice of the customer plan is designed to help organize the required elements when collecting voice of the customer data. The collection plan helps to highlight who should be represented in the data, how much data should be collected, what information should be collected, how and when the information will be collected, and who will collect the data. It also provides space to write down specific questions that could be used in the voice of the customer collection.

HOW TO COMPLETE:

1. Identify the customers or stakeholder groups that should be represented in the final voice of the customer data. Whose voice is important in understanding the current problem and the desired future state?

2. Determine the sample size needed to get a representative sample of voice of the customer data. (We will talk in-depth about sample size in the next chapter.)

3. Decide how the voice of the customer will be obtained. This may be done through a survey, focus group, or one-on-one interviews, etc.

4. Determine the timeframe for collecting the data. How long will you give people to complete the survey? How long would a focus group meet? What is the deadline for obtaining voice of the customer data to keep the project moving forward?

5. Assign responsibilities for collecting voice of the customer data to ensure that someone is accountable for this information.

6. Finally, use this information to start to develop specific questions for each customer group.

Tips:

- This is a good group activity to complete with the team to ensure that various points of view are considered. Consider drawing a grid on a white board or poster and writing in the information, or create a template in Microsoft Excel and type the information as you go.

- Think about the groups of customers that will be targeted. Are the groups different enough that they require different questions? Are there any customer or stakeholder groups that could be combined to utilize the same questions? Is it anticipated that the groups will have significantly different needs or very similar needs?

- When thinking about what to ask the customers, think about the charter. It is important to keep in mind the scope of the project when deciding what to ask customers. What questions will give you the most relevant information? How can some questions be phrased to keep customer responses in line with project goals?

- Sometimes voice of the customer data has already been collected via an institutional survey or by another group. Check to see if there is data relevant to the project that can be reused before collecting additional data.

Example:
Ophthalmology Clinic Flow

The Ophthalmology team created a VOC plan to hear from both staff and patients.

CUSTOMER GROUP	TARGET NUMBER OF RESPONSES	COLLECTION METHOD	TIMEFRAME FOR COLLECTION	RESPONSIBLE FOR COLLECTION	POSSIBLE QUESTIONS
Patients	50	Patient Experience Survey (pull report)	6 months	Erika to pull comments from report	The patient experience survey is already created. We will look at comments from the sections regarding access, clinic flow, and clinic environment
Retina Staff	10	Group Interview	1 hour	Joe to lead focus group session	1. What contributes to a positive day in the clinic? 2. What makes for a challenging day in clinic? 3. From a patient perspective, how does the clinic function?
Technicians	20	Survey	1 week	Nancy to create survey and send to techs	1. How would you describe clinic flow? 2. Do you feel that your team is dependable? Why or why not?

Once you have created the voice of the customer survey and executed on it, you should have valuable comments from your customers about the current process. This information is absolutely essential to have when working to improve the process. Without understanding what the customer wants, you might make changes that the team thinks are wonderful, only to find out that they do not address the needs of your customers.

If you did a survey, then you probably have verbatims (direct quotes) straight from the customers. If you did a focus group or interviews, then you likely have either verbatims or facilitator summaries of what customers said. You will have the best results if the comments that you work with are those direct verbatims from the customers. With this information gathered, you move on to step two of the VOC process: categorize feedback.

Categorize feedback

The goal of this second step is to take all of the feedback that you have received about your process and start to group it into categories or themes. This helps you to understand the common concerns or joys that patients have with the current process. An affinity diagram is a great tool that can help a team to take hundreds of individual comments and group them into themes in a very short period of time.

Tool: Affinity Diagram

PURPOSE: An affinity diagram helps a team gather and group the results of a voice of the customer survey (or brainstormed ideas in the Improve phase). It allows the team to take a large number of ideas or comments and then organize them into natural groupings or themes.

HOW TO COMPLETE:

1. Gather ideas or customer needs from interview transcripts, surveys, or other sources from your VOC process

2. Transfer the data onto index cards or sticky notes that can easily be moved around and grouped.

3. Group the notes together to find the common themes or groupings. This is typically done best as a silent group activity. Some comments may belong in multiple categories and it is okay to move cards among different categories.

4. For each grouping, label them with a common theme or driver.

5. If necessary, divide large groupings into subgroups and repeat the header process.

Tips:

- Try not to start with defined categories, let them emerge naturally.

- Sort in silence to help the team focus on the meaning behind and connections between the ideas or comments.

- It is okay for some notes to stand alone.

- Spend the extra time to construct themes that capture the essence of the groupings.

- Shortcuts greatly reduce the effectiveness of the affinity diagram.
- Ideas or comments are organized and clustered based on intuition or gut reaction.

Example:
Ophthalmology Clinic Flow Project

During the affinity diagram, it became clear to the Ophthalmology team that customers recognized an issue with delays in clinic and also a lack of standardization in many areas of practice.

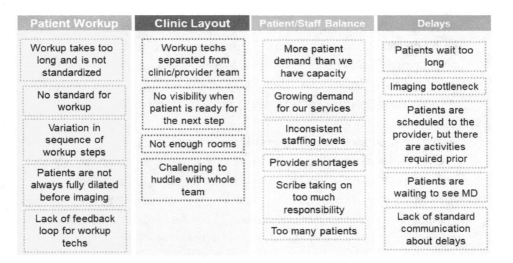

Patient Workup	Clinic Layout	Patient/Staff Balance	Delays
Workup takes too long and is not standardized	Workup techs separated from clinic/provider team	More patient demand than we have capacity	Patients wait too long
No standard for workup	No visibility when patient is ready for the next step	Growing demand for our services	Imaging bottleneck
Variation in sequence of workup steps	Not enough rooms	Inconsistent staffing levels	Patients are scheduled to the provider, but there are activities required prior
Patients are not always fully dilated before imaging	Challenging to huddle with whole team	Provider shortages	Patients are waiting to see MD
Lack of feedback loop for workup techs		Scribe taking on too much responsibility	Lack of standard communication about delays
		Too many patients	

Once you have categorized the customer feedback using the affinity diagram, it is time to translate that into something that you can measure throughout the course of your project, bringing us to the third step in the VOC process. But before you move on to that, take a moment and really reflect on the affinity diagram.

First, be proud of what your team accomplished – when you have dozens of comments to affinitize there is generally some skepticism on the team that this can be done in a one hour meeting or less, but it almost always is! I often like to watch a team do the affinity diagram to see how well they are currently functioning as a team. Did they fly through it with only civil discussion or were some people dominating the activity? This can tell you a lot as the team leader about how the dynamics of your team are currently structured so that you can consider those when facilitating other activities. Second, think about what the customers are telling you about the process. This is the time to really think about the process from the customer perspective. As staff and leaders, we often know that a process is broken and affecting our customers, but we still look at it through the lens of the business. Use this opportunity to put yourself in the customer's shoes – would you still feel the same way? Can you sympathize with aspects of their experience? Then, drop all the mushy emotional stuff and turn those comments into measurable characteristics.

Translate feedback into measurable characteristics

Creating measurable characteristics, or specifications, about what the customer wants from the process, allows us to collect data. Are we meeting any of their expectations? What is the gap between their expectations and our performance? This information can help to amend project goals and also guide data collection in the Measure phase. The tool to help you do this is called a CTx tree, which stands for "critical to x". The x is much like the x in algebra – it could stand for any number of things; quality, safety, patient experience, etc. During the categorizing step you took individual comments and grouped them into themes – these themes will be present in your

CTx tree, but you will also have to drill down to a more specific level to get the measurable specifications. These specifications will often come directly from the comments, sometimes word for word or sometimes a combination of a handful of comments.

Tool: CTx Tree (Critical to X)

PURPOSE: The CTx tree diagram is used to identify key measurable characteristics or features of products and services that are critical to an area of customer requirement. This may include quality, patient safety, revenue, etc.

HOW TO COMPLETE:

1. Gather customer or patient needs from the Voice of the Customer process or from a completed affinity diagram.

2. Decide on a general need (description of what the customer wants) and enter it in the far left column.

3. List the drivers of customer needs (the essential elements) in the middle column. These might be the categories from the affinity diagram.

4. Translate the customer feedback into measurable characteristics in the third column. For each driver ask the team what this means to the customer based on the responses that were collected. These should be measurable ways to determine if the driver is being achieved.

Tips:

- When thinking about the general need, keep in mind what it is that the customer wants or needs. This may be found from a persistent theme in the affinity diagram or from the goals on your project charter.

- Drivers are the inputs into the overall need and typically come directly from the themes discovered in the affinity diagram.

- If the team is struggling to translate a customer verbatim into a measurable action, think of switching a negative comment into a positive

  - Example: For "They are never on time", the CTx would be "Start on time". This is a measurable characteristic as one can determine how often something does or does not start on time.

- It can be helpful to prep the need and drivers in advance of a team meeting and focus on walking through the critical characteristics together.

- Do not feel like you need to include all themes from the affinity diagram. Typically, 2-3 is enough. Focus on themes that are within the scope of the project and are something that the team would have control over improving as you go forward.

Example:
Ophthalmology Clinic Flow

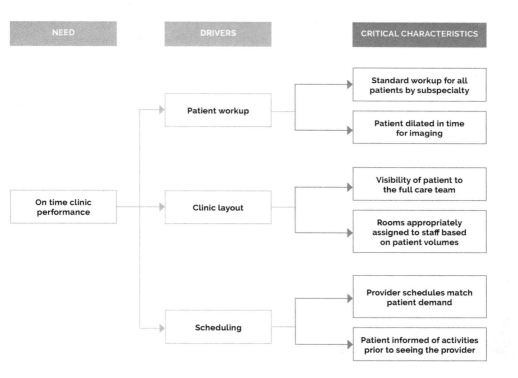

The critical characteristics that you have identified in the CTx tree really become the bridge from Define to Measure. These are the characteristics for which you want to obtain measurable specifications. In the Ophthalmology example, some of the measures are simple: did it happen? Was the patient dilated in time for imaging? Yes or no? We can count the total number of instances and get a percentage to understand how often this is happening. Other specifications are clearly indicated by a number. In Ophthalmology we had a specification from patients that they wanted to spend no more than two hours in clinic from start to finish. These measurable specifications tell us what patients want and during Measure we can assess the current process to see if we are meeting them.

Once you have completed the CTx tree, you are ready to move from the Define phase to the Measure phase. As you close out each phase, best practice is to schedule a meeting with your sponsor to go over the team's work thus far and discuss plans for the upcoming phase. To prepare for this, review your charter and make sure it is reflective of all that you have learned during the Define phase. Here are some suggested questions to ask yourself at the end of the phase and to discuss with your sponsor:

- What is the problem we are trying to solve?
- Who are the stakeholders in this process?
- What is the business case and how does it link to our overall strategy?
- What are the measurable customer specifications?
- Has the sponsor approved the charter?
- Do you have the right people on the team and are they engaged?
- Is the scope of the work achievable?
- Is this work worth continuing?

If you feel like you have adequate answers to these questions, then go on! Move to the next phase. What are you waiting for? All of the fun happens in Measure!

Chapter Three:
Measure

The second phase in a DMAIC project is the Measure phase. This is when it is time to unleash your inner math nerd and really start to understand the current state of your process. If you don't have an inner math nerd, then find one you can borrow (don't actually borrow a person- that's weird. Just tap into the data energy of a team member). The goal of the measure phase is to understand current state. In order to get a complete picture of the current state of a process, we recommend that you think about the phase in three sections: data collection, visualizing the data, and visualizing the process. Measure really takes us from qualitative information (like what we gathered in the VOC work) and starts to shift our focus to more quantitative information. Both are absolutely essential in truly understanding a problem and a process.

DATA COLLECTION

When we are working with students, it is not uncommon for them to get to the Measure phase and look at us with their heads tilted like confused puppies. "What now?" At this point you understand a lot about your problem and your customers, but you don't really understand the current state of the process. Trying to determine where to start can be really challenging. Some days I wonder if this is even harder for the people closest to the process – you work in it every day and it can be challenging to identify aspects of it that should be measured for more understanding.

In addition, you may have people on your team (yourself included) who don't really think that gathering data is all that important. You work in the process; therefore, you know what is happening, right? There is a good chance that you feel like this is the case; we feel that way too sometimes. Unfortunately, in reality, people's confidence that they know what the problem is has no link to them actually being correct about the problem. Data is essential in helping to remove emotions from decision-making and ensuring that we aren't making unwarranted assumptions. Sometimes when you collect data, that data will validate what you thought to be true of the process, but at least as often it will not. This is why we have to collect it! It is the most objective way to paint a picture of current state.

We need to understand current state for a couple of reasons. First, because if you can't measure a problem, then how can you possibly improve it? You need to be able to assess current state as compared with customer specifications and/or your overall project goals and objectives. You also need to take a baseline measurement of current state. This tells you how the process is performing today. This is needed for comparison with the future state. After improvements have been made, you can compare data about the process from before and after improvements to understand the true impact of your efforts.

Take a look at your CTx tree. This can be a great starting point to decide what to measure. It might indicate specifications for the length of an appointment or the acceptable wait time before a visit. It might have other specifications that can be measured in a yes/no fashion where you can understand the proportion of the time that the specifications are met. Another way to identify places to collect data is during direct observation of the process. As a project leader, you should always plan to observe the process. This is one of the most valuable components of process improvement work. Observing the process from the outside (even if it is a process you are very familiar with) can give all sorts of insights. This is especially true of having fresh eyes on a process. It is often very useful to have team members observe parts of the process that they are not typically responsible for completing. This gives good insight into what other team members do in the process and also helps to identify areas where data could be collected to better understand the process. This approach provides team members with the opportunity to walk in each other's shoes.

In order to plan appropriately for data collection, there are a few (only a few, I promise!) concepts that we should explore. I know you didn't buy a math textbook, so we will try to keep this quick and straight to the point – this information is really important to keep in mind when collecting data.

Operational Definition

Operational definition is a term given to a precise description of a metric. We might establish a metric of "patient wait time", but this could mean different things to different people. One might consider wait time from the time that the patient arrives until they are seen by the provider. Another might consider wait time from the time that the patient was scheduled to see the provider until they are roomed by the medical assistant. Operational definitions help to remove ambiguity so that everyone has the same understanding of what each metric means. While this might seem unnecessary in some cases, it is actually needed a lot more often than you would expect. Without a clear operational definition, people might collect data in different ways which can have a significant impact on the quality and the validity of your data.

We know this to be true, because over the years, we have learned from our own mistakes. Let's talk through an example from one of our author's early DMAIC projects. A group of secretaries were asked to collect data on the amount of time that they spent working on each outpatient referral in their clinic. The data was being collected to better understand the amount of active time that secretaries spent getting a referral scheduled and how much of that time was spent on the phone with a patient or tracking down previous medical information from other providers. The directions given to the secretaries were to write down when they started working on a referral and when they stopped working on the referral. They were asked to document this for each referral, each time they worked on it. When the data was collected by the project leader, it was clear that the secretaries had made different assumptions about the instructions. Two secretaries wrote down the exact minute that they started working on the referral and the exact minute that they stopped. However, one secretary rounded everything to the nearest five minute interval. Since most of the time secretaries were only working on a referral for 15 minutes or less at a given time, this ended up impacting the quality of the total data set. The project leader could not use information collected by that secretary because there was no way to understand if she was rounding up or down or by how much. With a more precise operational definition of what the project leader was looking for, this could have been avoided.

When we as project leaders and team members collect data or ask the staff that we work with to collect data about a process, we want to make sure to respect the time that they spend doing so. If we have to throw out a bunch of that data because we didn't give a clear definition of what needed to be collected up front, that isn't very respectful and could discourage staff from participating in the future. Not to mention, if you then need to spend a few weeks recollecting the data, this is also going to severely impact your project timeline.

Sampling

After coming up with your clear operational definition, you should then start to think about where the data is going to come from. Is the data available via an electronic report that can be pulled from a system (EMR, payroll, patient experience or employee engagement survey)? Or is the data something that would need to be manually collected? In a lot of projects, it is common to see both situations arise. Often it is possible to get some data from a system, but it is rare that you can get all of the information that you need without manually collecting data as well.

With both data collection methods, you are probably going to employ a technique called sampling. Sampling simply refers to the process of taking a subset of data and using that to draw conclusions about the whole population or process. We sample because it would not be feasible to capture every single data point in a population due to time, money, and resources. Sampling is especially important when you are manually collecting data, as you want to collect enough data to draw meaningful conclusions without overburdening the staff that are collecting the data.

The key thing about sampling is to make sure that our sample is representative of the overall process or population. If we do not have a representative sample, then we might have what is called sampling bias. This bias could cause us to draw conclusions about the larger process or population that may not be accurate. Bias most often occurs when we sample based on data that is convenient for us to collect. For example, if I want to collect data on patient wait times in a clinic and I only collect data on Monday mornings from 8:00AM – 10:00AM or Friday afternoons from 2:00PM – 4:00PM, because that is when I have time available on my calendar, I am likely to get a pretty biased sample. The wait times experienced on a Monday morning or Friday afternoon might be very different than what is experienced on a Wednesday at 1:00PM. It is for this reason that we need to purposefully try to collect a representative sample and target our data collection approaches.

In ensuring a representative sample, we need to think about two larger bodies: the population and the process. Most improvement projects are focused on improving a process, so it is usually elements of a process that we consider most important when selecting our samples. However, for some projects, it might also be important to look at the patient population as a group and make sure that we sample them in a representative way. Use the chart below to understand the difference between sampling a process and sampling a population.

	PROCESS	POPULATION
Definition of Sampling	Selecting a subset of data, measuring certain characteristics, and then making inferences about how a system is performing (this could be data about people but the focus is on the process, not characteristics of the people)	Selecting a subset of people, measuring certain characteristics, and then making inferences about that population as a whole
Example	Looking at patient wait times in a clinic for 1 week, to understand the average patient wait experience in that clinic	Looking at addresses for patients at the hospital who have been seen in the last year to determine where the hospital's patient population lives

We can use different sampling techniques to improve our chances of obtaining a representative sample:

- **Random sampling:** every data point has an equal chance of being selected for the sample (might use a random number generator)
- **Stratified random sampling:** the population is broken into groups and random samples are drawn to match the total population of these groups (could be male/female, insurance payer, or Primary Care Provider)
- **Subgroup sampling:** selecting a certain number of samples for a given time period (selecting x number of patients per day)
- **Systematic sampling:** sample a patient at predetermined intervals (every other patient, or every third patient). *Watch out for this one if you are working on a process where predetermined templates are used. For example, if your providers see a new patient, then a follow-up, then a new, and so-on, you could be missing an entire visit type when capturing information about the flow of the clinic.*

Each of these sampling techniques has benefits and drawbacks, the key with sampling is to try to get as diverse a sample as necessary to truly draw conclusions about the larger process or population. In order to do this, you also need to make sure that the sample size is appropriate. I would love to tell you that there is a perfect way to calculate the sample size that you should collect, but that just isn't the reality of the situation. Figuring out the correct sample size depends on a lot of factors, especially when you have to manually collect data in addition to your typical work responsibilities. Here are some factors to consider when thinking about a sample size:

- Ease of access to the data – if you are pulling data from a system and you can capture large amounts of data with the click of a button, then more is definitely better.
- Variation in the process – if you have a process that is showing a lot of variation, you probably need to collect more data to get an accurate picture. (We will talk about histograms later in this chapter, but if the shape of your histogram continues to change when new data is added, keep collecting data until it remains relatively stable.)
- Breaking the data into groups – if you are going to separate the data by provider, sub-specialty service, procedure, or some other factor, you need to make sure that you have a sufficient number of data points for each of those categories – which means collecting more data points overall.
- Rarity of the events – some events in healthcare are rare and it can be difficult to collect large numbers of data points (this is a good thing, though!!). For example, hospital-acquired conditions do not occur at high frequencies, a few a month is substantial. In those instances, you may need to look at data over longer periods of time or consider "non-instances" as a comparison point. Instead of looking at the total number of CLABSI (central-line) infections each month, look at the number of infections compared to the number of patients

with a central line and no infections that month. This will also account for the change in patients with a central line from month to month and be more accurate than simply counting the volume of central line infections.

While it pains us to even give you an actual number, because there is so much to consider, we will say this: as a general rule of thumb, please do not try to draw conclusions if you have less than 30 data points. That is rarely enough to understand what is really happening in a process. Use good judgement though – if you see 200 patients a day and you are collecting data for five days, you should definitely be collecting more than 30 data points!

Stratification and Disaggregation

Before settling on a sample size and a sampling technique, it can be helpful to consider a couple of other factors: stratification and disaggregation.

Stratification is something that we have already alluded to. It is the process of taking your data and breaking it into groups or sub-groups based on certain characteristics. By separating the data into these groups, we are considering variables that might account for some of the variation in a group. For example, if I am looking at data on performance in the operating room, it might be helpful for me to break that information into categories based on the clinical service (see image). Knowing how I may want to group my data helps to ensure that I collect a large enough sample size, and capture that information when I am collecting the data. In this case, I would need to have the clinical service included on a system report or written down during manual data collection, and it is always best to be aware of that information upfront rather than after you've put a lot of work into data collection.

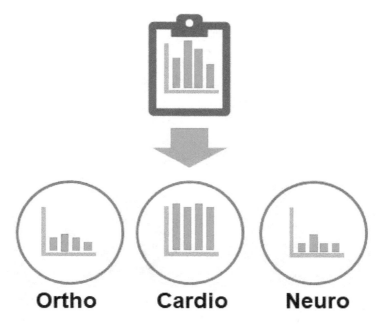

Ortho   Cardio   Neuro

Disaggregation is a similar concept. Typically, when we review process data we view it in an aggregated or "rolled-up" format. We can take this information and break it into smaller pieces to learn more information. For example, if I want to understand patient wait time in a clinic, I can calculate their total wait time only, or I can capture time stamps that reflect smaller parts of the process. This allows me to review the process in greater detail or in an aggregated format that shows total wait time. Review the image to see how wait time could be further disaggregated. Knowing how data, especially time-related data, might be disaggregated to give you more information can be really helpful to know upfront. If you collect data on wait times but do not break this down from the beginning, you might not have the information you want when you go to analyze the information later.

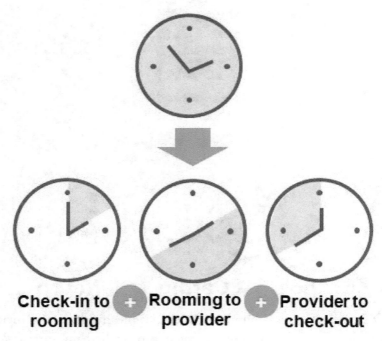

By now you've probably been thinking about so many aspects of the data that you want to collect that you have a headache. Well, we've got good news! We have a plan for this too! No need to try to keep all this information in your head, you can use a data collection plan to help think about each of these components for all of the data that you need to collect.

Tool: Data Collection Plan

PURPOSE: The data collection plan is designed to organize all of the information that is needed to begin the data collection process in a project.

HOW TO COMPLETE:

1. **Metric:** Think about the different variables or metrics that should be captured to help understand current state. List each of these separately in the first column of the data collection plan. These measures might have been identified earlier in the project while working on voice of the customer data or flowcharting the current process.

2. **Operational Definition:** Develop a specific and complete definition for the measurement. Ensure that this definition is agreed upon by the team and fully understood by everyone who will be collecting the data.

3. **Measurement Method and Source:** Determine how the variable will be measured. What instrument will be used? Where will this data come from? Can the information be pulled from a system report or does it need to be manually collected?

4. **Sample Size:** Indicate the total number of data points to be collected and the details of any necessary stratification. Will the sample be representative? How might observations need to be staggered to ensure a representative sample?

5. **Timeframe or Frequency:** Define the timeframe for which the data will be collected. If running a report, what timeframe will be looked at? If doing observations, how frequently will observations occur and for what length of time? When should all data collection be completed?

6. **Responsibility:** Indicate the person or people responsible for collecting the data.

Tips:

- When working through the data collection plan it is important for the team to consider some of the contextual information that might also be relevant and useful when trying to understand the data. For example, one might want demographic information about the patients to be able to stratify that data based on patient location or age.

- Before implementing the data collection plan in full and collecting all of the data, it is useful to validate the plan. Collect a small, but representative sample, of the data to ensure that when collected according to the plan, the data coming back is the intended measurement target.

- When multiple people are involved in collecting the data, it is important to think about inter-rater reliability. Are the different raters coming up with the same results for the same measurement? Is there a difference in the data resulting from the way that they are collecting the data, rather than from an actual observed difference? (You'll see more about this shortly.)

Example:

Ophthalmology Clinic Flow

METRIC: WHAT DATA IS COLLECTED?	OPERATIONAL DEFINITION	MEASUREMENT METHOD AND SOURCE: HOW IS THE MEASUREMENT MADE AND WHERE DOES IT COME FROM?	SAMPLE SIZE: HOW MUCH DATA IS COLLECTED?	TIMEFRAME OR FREQUENCY OF MEASUREMENT	RESPONSIBILITY: WHO COLLECTS THE DATA?
Appointment cycle time	Total time from patient appointment time to patient check-out	Ophthalmology technicians will capture this information in the EMR	All patients for a 2 week period	Daily	All Ophthalmology technicians
Patient satisfaction with wait time	Patient response to standard patient experience survey question #18	Patients fill out satisfaction surveys after their visit, data is compiled monthly and sent to section leadership	All patient survey responses from the last 6 months	Data collected retroactively for the last 6 months	Operations manager
Appointment volumes by day	Number of provider visits and scheduled imaging appointments each day	Data is pulled from the EMR via the scheduling system	All patient appointments from the last 12 months	Data collected retroactively for the last 12 months	Administrative supervisor

When manually collecting data, it can be helpful to create data collection forms for use. Whether you are collecting all the data yourself (don't do that!), your team members are helping (Yay, team members!), or you're asking the staff who do the work to assist, having a form can ensure that everyone is collecting the same data and capturing all of the data needed for each instance. Without a data collection form of some kind, you might miss pieces of information when you get busy observing and collecting.

Data collection forms can be created simply and quickly. You can use a spreadsheet or a word processing document to create something simple, like a table, or you can create more of a fill in the blank or tick and tally type form. Create something that will work for the data collectors and help you organize the data easily after the collection period. While some free text can be helpful for comments that provide context, remember that too much free text can be difficult to summarize and analyze later on.

It is also important that data collected is both valid and reliable. Validity is when a measurement system measures what it is intended to measure. An example of this would be pulling data on total appointment cycle time from the electronic medical record. I can pull the patient arrival time and the time that the encounter was closed by the provider. If I pull these numbers, I can calculate the duration of the appointment. However, if my providers are not closing their appointment encounters until after the patient has left because they are still working on their documentation, then that data would not be valid. It is not actually measuring what I am intending to measure, which is the duration that the patient is present for the appointment. Reliability is when a measurement system consistently produces the same result. This is a different concept, this looks more at repeatability. If I pull those same two time stamps from the medical record, are they pulling from the same two fields every time? If not, there is a problem with the reliability of the report. You might get information from the right source or you might not. This has nothing to do with if the measurement is valid because you could be reliably getting invalid data if the time stamps are pulling from the same location each time, but that location is capturing an encounter that is closed hours after the visit.

These are important factors to remember for both electronic data reports and manual data collection. With manual data collection, we often think about inter-rater reliability. When you have multiple people collecting data, it is important to ensure that they are capturing it in the same way. To help with this you can use clear operational definitions, data collection forms, and check-in on staff during the data collection period to see how they are doing and if they have any questions about data collection.

Inter-rater reliability and other forms of measurement systems analysis (a fancy term for making sure that your measurement system is valid and reliable) are topics that can get very complex as you think about increasing the statistical rigor around them. They are important concepts, but are also challenging to implement in a healthcare setting. We recommend you do your best to validate your data and train data collectors appropriately. It can help to compare electronically reported data to observations and anecdotal comments. It is also beneficial to check in with staff regularly when they are collecting data. Evaluate the data as you go and make sure you are capturing what you need. Discuss common data collection errors and help staff find ways to avoid making those errors. The more involved you are throughout the data collection process, the better your chances of securing good data for your project. It is much better to throw out two days' worth of data because you noticed some inconsistencies or errors, than two weeks of data because you waited until the end to review.

VISUALIZE THE DATA

This next section is all about summarizing the data, ideally into pictures! Pictures aren't so bad, right? Before we start showing you all the data-related pictures though, we do need to go over a little bit more terminology and conceptual information. It is all important information when it comes to understanding your data, choosing the appropriate visualization tools, and for analyzing the data in detail. If you are starting to get bored with all of our math gibberish, put the book down and do 20 jumping jacks, then come back and power through these last few concepts because you are already almost through the densest part of the book.

Types of Data

There are two types of data and it is important to differentiate between the two: continuous and discrete. Continuous data is numerical data that can be represented by fractions or decimal points. The most common example of this in healthcare is time. You can have 1.2 minutes, 1.4 minutes, or 1.6 minutes. Other examples include age, height, and weight. Discrete data is numerical data that contains only whole numbers (typically count data), percentages, or categorical data. Categorical data is easy – think anything with words! This could be gender, insurance payer, or visit type. Count data is represented by whole numbers because we can't have a fractional amount of it. For example, if we are counting the number of patient infections, you can't have 1.2 infections or 1.4 infections; you either have 1 infection or you have 2 infections. Percentages are an interesting one. You can have percentages with decimal points, so sometimes this throws people for a loop. Instead of thinking about percentages as numbers that have decimal points, think about them as proportions. A percentage is derived from one number divided by another number. Those numbers are from discrete data. If we divide a discrete number by another discrete number, it can't magically morph into a continuous data point – even if it is now a percentage with a decimal point. If you're still confused about percentages, just trust us (we haven't led you astray yet!), they're definitely discrete. Knowing whether you have discrete or continuous data is really important when you are using descriptive statistics or visualizing your data with charts and graphs.

Measures of Central Tendency and Dispersion

As a refresher, we are going to introduce some basic statistics. Measures of central tendency were probably covered somewhere in your past, but if you haven't used them, there is a good chance that the reminder will be helpful. You may or may not have been exposed to measures of dispersion before, but they are often paired with measures of central tendency to help summarize a data set.

Mean, median, and mode are the three measures of central tendency that we are going to cover. Each of these statistics helps us to understand the center of our data. Now, understanding the center of a data set might look different depending on the distribution of the data set (which we will cover in more detail next). Use the chart below to review the definition, benefits and drawbacks, and some healthcare examples for each of the three statistics.

	DEFINITION	BENEFITS/DRAWBACKS	EXAMPLES
Mean	The average of all data points calculated by adding each value and dividing by the number of data points	+ Takes into account all data values + Can be used for mathematical operations - Affected by extreme values (outliers) - Cannot be located quickly at a glance in a non-symmetrical distribution - Gives misleading conclusions if data is not normally distributed	• Average turnaround time • Average patient wait time • Average case mix index
Median	The middle value of a data set when all values are arranged in order	+ Can be determined quickly, even with extreme values + Can be located graphically - Harder to calculate than the mean - Not capable of further mathematical treatment - In the case of an even number of values it may not be a value from the data set	• Median length of stay • Median time from referral to appointment
Mode	The value of a data set that occurs most frequently	+ Not affected by extreme values + Easy to determine visually + Often an important value to describe the data - Not capable of further mathematical treatment - Not based on individual data points - Choice of grouping can have a great influence on the value	• Most common visit type • Most common planned appointment time

When you are collecting data about a process, it isn't very helpful to only look at each individual data point. You want to be able to see the full picture. Using measures of central tendency will start to give you a better idea about the typical performance of the process. That picture becomes even clearer when you also look at a measure of dispersion. Measures of dispersion help us to understand the spread of a data set, or the variation. We will talk more about variation later on, but when it comes to measures of dispersion, remember that the larger the number, the more variation is present in the process. Below is a chart that describes range, interquartile range, and standard deviation.

	DEFINITION	BENEFITS/DRAWBACKS	EXAMPLES
Range	The difference between the largest and smallest data point	+ Very easy to calculate and provide a number that tells you how spread out a data set is - Largely affected by the presence of outliers - Ignores all data values except the largest and smallest data point	• Range of patient acuity levels • Range of actual appointment durations
Interquartile range (IQR)	The difference between the third quartile and the first quartile – provides a range for the middle-half of the values in a data set	+ Less sensitive to outliers than the range + Can be easy to calculate if data points are in numerical order - Only looks at the middle 50% of the data and could be excluding important information from the other 50%	• IQR for hospital inpatient age at time of admission • IQR for employee engagement scores
Standard deviation (SD)	The average distance of each data point from the mean	+ Helps to make the mean more useful by providing additional information about the dispersion of the data set + Strongest way to measure variation in a data set - Doesn't tell you the full range of the data - Difficult to calculate by hand	• SD in HbA1c levels for diabetic patients managed by primary care • SD in wait times for OB ultrasound

None of these values needs to be calculated by hand, unless you really want to practice your manual math skills. If you have Microsoft Excel, there are functions available to calculate these values for any data range. Use the function library in Excel to find the ones most appropriate for your needs.

Calculating descriptive statistics is important for providing a baseline for us to understand our data. They might help to spark additional questions about the data or the process. But they will be most helpful when also paired with a visual of the data. That old adage about a picture being worth a thousand words is definitely true when it comes to looking at data. No one wants to look line-by-line through a spreadsheet of data to understand a process (not even us, and we really like our spreadsheets!).

There are a lot of data visualization options out there, but we are going to focus on the ones that are most utilized in Lean Six Sigma and that have proven invaluable in our healthcare work. The first of which are histograms. Histograms are one type of frequency plot that are perfect for understanding how frequently various data values occur in a data set. Histograms can only be used with continuous data, but they very quickly show us the mode (the highest point on the graph), the center of our data, and the range or distribution of the data. There are common shapes seen in frequency plots that can help us to start to understand the process or raise specific questions about what we are seeing.

Take a look at the tool first, and then we will discuss some of the common shapes that you might see and what to consider when reacting to them.

Tool: Histogram

PURPOSE: A histogram is used to graphically represent the spread and frequency distribution of data. A histogram is a type of frequency plot that graphs occurrence like a bar chart. Data is grouped into classes that represent the frequency of data within a range rather than being graphed individually. A histogram works best to display large amounts of data (typically greater than 50 points).

HOW TO COMPLETE:

1. Using Microsoft Excel, with the SPC XL add-in enabled, set up the data in a column. If the data is already in a workbook in one column, this can be done from the original workbook.

2. Click on the "SigmaZone" tab at the top, select the "Analysis Diagrams" dropdown menu, then choose "Histogram".

3. A box will pop up asking for the data range for the histogram. Select the appropriate range – this should be all of the values for one measurement. It is okay to select the title and/or to have blank cells within the selection range. Click "Next".

4. Another pop up box will appear called "Histogram Options". Here different aspects of the histogram can be edited before it is created. See below for details of these options and once complete, click "Finish".

   a. **Anchor Point:** This is the starting variable for the data. It will default to the lowest number in the set but can be edited to start lower if desired (i.e. to keep the scale the same as another data set that may have had a smaller data point value).

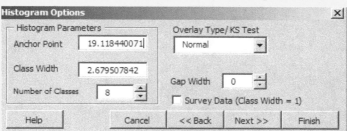

b. **Class Width:** This determines the range of values to be included in each histogram "bucket". If too many values are in each range, you can adjust this by narrowing the range per class.

c. **Number of Classes:** Similar to class width, this also changes the way the histogram "buckets" are distributed. The number of classes can be changed using this feature (best to use in conjunction with class width to ensure that the appropriate number of classes and the ranges within each class are appropriate).

d. **Overlay Type/KS Test:** This feature puts an overlay line on top of the histogram which can help to visualize the type of distribution present. The most common choice here is the "normal" distribution overlay, which helps to visually see if the data is normally distributed. The overlay line can also be turned off in this dropdown.

e. **Gap Width:** This adjusts the spacing between the bars of the histogram. The default is for the bars to be touching, but the gap width can be increased to separate them for aesthetic purposes.

Tips:

- The histogram feature in SPC XL will also cal-culate the mean and standard deviation for the plotted data set. These are numbers that might be useful in explaining the data set, especially if it is normally distributed.

- Histograms are used when the measured vari-able is continuous (i.e. temperature, time, weight, speed, etc.). If looking at discrete data (categor-ical answers, yes/no, etc.), it is more appropriate to use a standard bar graph.

- The histogram distribution will be most repre-sentative of the overall population with a large and representative sample size. To really ana-lyze the distribution pattern and make decisions with a histogram it is best to have at least 50 data points included.

- Note: Histograms can be created in almost any statistical software, there are even ways to do this in Excel without the SPC XL add-in package. Look at your specific software for information about how to set up the data.

Example:
Pathway to Discharge

Below is the histogram for PACU boarding time used by the Pathway to Discharge team. The horizontal axis shows time in minutes and the vertical access shows frequency of occurrence. We can see that most patients are waiting in the PACU for 0-55 minutes, while some patients had much longer boarding times.

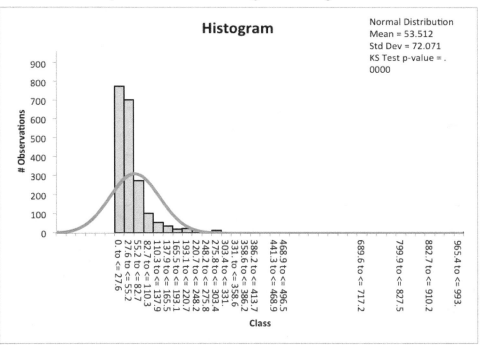

The shape of a histogram tells us a lot. In the example histogram, we can see that there is a really wide range of times associated with boarding in the Post-Acute Care Unit (from 0-993 minutes). The team started by investigating the longer boarding times to better understand what was making those cases so different from the typical experience. Use the next chart to look at some common histogram patterns and get an idea for what steps to take when you see these patterns.

VISUAL EXAMPLE OF SHAPE	NAME/ DESCRIPTION	CONCLUSION	ACTION
	Bell shaped (Normal Distribution)	There is no special cause variation indicated by the distribution (Note: special causes might be identified using a time plot or control chart.)	Make changes aimed at improving the overall process (not focused on special causes). It is safe to use most statistical calculations with normal data.
	Long tail (Skewed Distribution)	The data in this process *might* have a cut-off point. For example, when using time on the X-axis, it cannot take less than 0 hours to complete a task. This creates a boundary on the left side of your data which often contributes to the skew.	Use caution when working with most statistical calculations. Control charts, hypothesis tests, and regression rely on normal data distributions. Use the median to describe this data set.
	Bimodal	The data might be representing more than one process. For example, in looking at time to clean hospital rooms, you might be looking at the night shift and day shift as one data set, when they actually represent two different processes that perform differently.	Stratify your data in a different way to understand what might be causing the bimodal distribution. Be wary of using control charts or time plots until the data has been stratified.

VISUAL EXAMPLE OF SHAPE	NAME/ DESCRIPTION	CONCLUSION	ACTION
	Basically flat	The process may be a mix of many operating conditions (and have multiple factors affecting the results).	Use time plots to track over time. Look for possible ways to stratify the data. Standardize the process.
	One or more outliers	Outlier data points could be the result of a measurement error or something unusual that happened in the process.	Confirm that outliers were not due to measurement error and then treat like a special cause (coming soon!)

Before moving on to the next visualization option, we should spend a little bit more time on the normal distribution. The normal distribution is one that has special properties that make it mathematically unique. As we learn new tools, we will talk about some that assume your data is normal (if it's not, that is okay, but knowing this is important to understanding how the tool works).

The normal distribution is also commonly referred to as a "bell curve". The normal distribution is unique in that the mean, median, and mode are all equal and are located perfectly in the center of the data. The shape on either side of the mean is symmetrical. The area under the curve represents 100% of the data values. A normal distribution can be described using only the mean and the standard deviation. The mean tells us the location of the center of the data, and the standard deviation tells us the width of the distribution. Look at the next picture for a visual. Looking across, the means are the same, but looking vertically the standard deviations are the same. This helps to understand how these two numbers can be used to describe any normal data set.

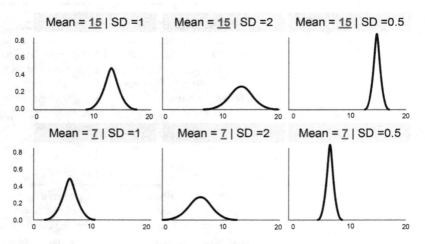

You might remember when we talked about mean, median, and mode earlier that we talked about how the mean is sensitive to all data values, whereas the median is not. This is why it is important to use the mean to describe any data that is normal, but the mean might be a misleading option for data sets that appear in the other shapes we discussed (especially the long-tailed distribution). This is because the mean will be pulled to the end of the distribution that has more extreme data values, even if that is not the most common data point. Look at the picture below for a visual.

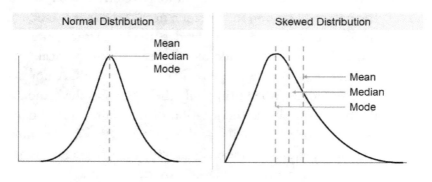

Another important characteristic about normal data is the empirical rule. The empirical rule states that with normal data, the following data distribution will occur: 68% of data points will occur within 1 standard deviation (plus or minus) of the mean, 95% of data points will occur within 2 standard deviations of the mean, and 99.5% of data points will occur within 3 standard deviations of the mean. This will be important when we talk about some of the rules associated with control charts later in this chapter.

Now you have an idea of what a normal distribution looks like and why it is important to assess your data set to determine if it is normal. It is also important to note that you may have a normal distribution, but that might not always be obvious just by looking at it. Earlier we talked about sample size and I indicated that watching the shape of your distribution can be important. If you have a sample size of 50 and see a bimodal distribution, but add another 25 data points and start to see that distribution more closely resemble a normal distribution, you should probably continue collecting data until the shape stabilizes. For this reason, and others, it is possible to have data that is normally distributed without realizing it. Many statistical programs have a normality test built in. In SPC XL, the KS test (Kolmogorov-Smirnov Test) is included in the creation of each histogram and can help you determine if your data is normally distributed regardless of how it appears.

Tool: KS Test

PURPOSE: The normality test is used to determine how closely a given data set resembles a normal distribution. The assumption that a distribution is normal is important for many statistical calculations (and required for a few). The Kolmogorov-Smirnov Test (KS Test) is one normality test that can be used in SPC XL to assess the normality of a data set.

HOW TO COMPLETE:

1. Using Microsoft Excel, with the SPC XL add-in enabled, set up the data in a column. If the data is already in a workbook in one column, this can be done from the original workbook.

2. Click on the "SigmaZone" tab at the top, select the "Analysis Diagrams" dropdown menu, then choose "Histogram".

3. A box will pop up asking for the data range for the histogram. Select the appropriate range – this should be all of the values for one measurement. It is okay to select the title and/or to have blank cells within the selection range. Click "Next".

4. Another pop up box will appear called "Histogram Options". Here different aspects of the histogram can be edited before it is created. Make sure that the "Normal" option is selected for "Overlay Type/KS Test". This will calculate the normality of the data. Click "Finish".

5. The KS Test p-value will appear on the histogram with other summary statistics.

Tips:

- The KS Test uses the null hypothesis that the data set is a normally distributed set of data. A p-value greater than 0.05 retains the null hypothesis which means that the data are normally distributed. A p-value less than 0.05 would reject the null hypothesis and indicate that the distribution is not normal. (We will learn all about p-values in Analyze.)

- Note: many programs can run the KS normality test. Review your software to determine how to run this or other tests for normality. Other statistical tests that assess normality include: Shapiro-Wilk and Anderson-Darling.

Example:
Pathway to Discharge

In looking at the histogram that we created for the PACU boarding time, we can see both visually and mathematically that this is not a normally distributed data set.

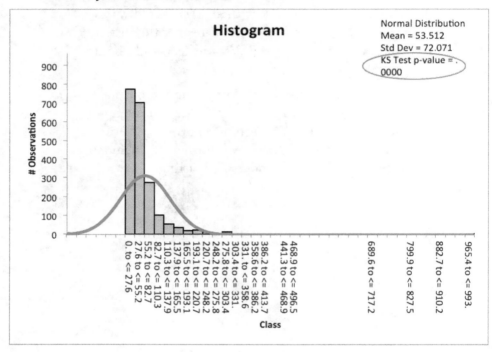

While you can get a lot of information about your data set from a histogram (and should definitely use it to check for normality), there are also other ways to visualize data that can give you additional information. If you have time ordered data, you can use a run chart or a control chart to learn more about patterns that might have emerged related to time. Time-ordered data is anything that is collected at regular intervals: daily, weekly, monthly, hourly, etc. If you have time-ordered data and you use a histogram, you might get good information, but you might also miss out on patterns that could be related to the time. For instance, if I am looking at volume of phone calls received per hour, I might find that our highest volume of calls occurs daily from 10AM-1PM. On a histogram, I would not be able to tell specifically when high call volumes occur, just that they are present.

Run charts and control charts are a little different, so it is important to look at their similarities and differences. Note that control charts have more statistical rigor and should be used when higher levels of certainty are needed. A histogram shows the spread of data on the horizontal axis, but on a time plot, it is the vertical access that shows us the center of our data (median for a run chart, and mean for a control chart), and the spread of our distribution. Look at the picture below for an idea of how the two displays relate.

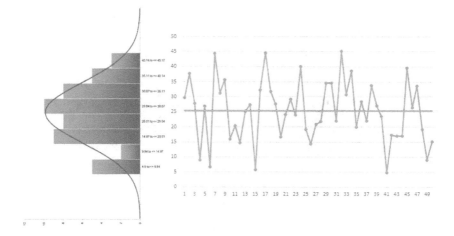

Time plots can be used with continuous data or discrete count data. We find them most useful for helping us to better understand variation in a process. First, let's look at a run chart and then some common patterns that might be found on a run chart. Then we will dive deeper into variation and utilize the control chart for mathematically understanding variation.

Tool: Run Chart

PURPOSE: A run chart is typically used to identify patterns of variation in a process, to monitor process performance, or to evaluate progress after a process change or improvement has been made. Run charts are a good way to visualize variation in a process and to recognize trends or shifts in a process. Run charts are used for time ordered data. They should not be used to look at data that does not have a time-related component.

HOW TO COMPLETE:

1. Using Microsoft Excel, set up the data in two columns (time period in one and variable data in the other). If the data is already in a workbook in two columns, this can be done from the original workbook.

2. Highlight both columns of data and click on the "Insert" tab at the top, select the 2D Line Chart option.

3. To display the median of the data set on the run chart, another column needs to be added before creating the chart. In the column next to the raw data, use the =MEDIAN function in Excel to determine the median and then populate that value for the entire column.

4. To create a chart with the median, select all three columns of data when selecting the range for the line chart.

5. Title the chart and add labels to both the vertical and horizontal axes.

Tips:

- In order to be able to spot trends and patterns, it is important to have enough data points. At least 24 are needed to deduce any meaningful patterns.

- The data should be set up in Excel in order from earliest to latest.

- When interpreting a run chart, look for the shape to determine if there are any shifts, trends, or other time-related patterns.

Example:
Ophthalmology Clinic Flow

The Ophthalmology project team collected data on total cycle time. This data was able to be disaggregated to look at individual components of the process. During observations, team members noticed that patients often had long waits before their imaging was completed and wanted to look at wait time prior to imaging specifically. They used a run chart to look at the average wait time for imaging for 24 weeks of data.

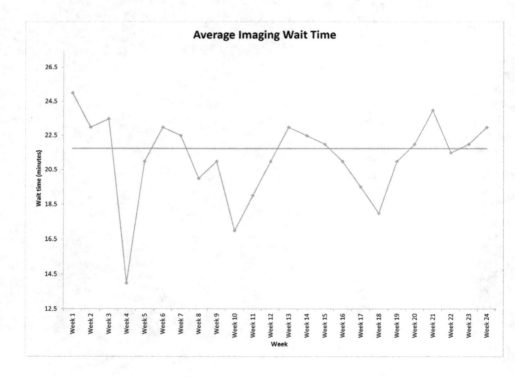

Now let's review some of the common shapes of run charts and determine how we might interpret those.

VISUAL EXAMPLE OF SHAPE	NAME/ DESCRIPTION	CONCLUSION	ACTION
	Trend: at least 6 points in a row, increasing or decreasing	Something in the process likely changed at the start of the trend.	Determine if this is a good trend or a bad trend. Investigate the point in time when the trend started and try to determine its cause.
	Shift: at least 8 points in a row, above or below the median	Something in the process likely changed at the start of the shift.	Determine if this is a good shift or a bad shift. Investigate the point in time when the shift occurred and try to determine its cause.
	Too Few Runs	This typically looks like shifts going back and forth across the median. Similar to your analysis of a bimodal distribution in a histogram, there could be different processes occurring here at different times. For example, the wait time for an appointment in the summer months, might be higher than the winter months.	Look at the time related pattern that you are seeing – is it related to time of day? Time of year? Determine the pattern shown and then brainstorm possible causes for the pattern. Evaluate to determine if those possible causes are accurate.

VISUAL EXAMPLE OF SHAPE	NAME/ DESCRIPTION	CONCLUSION	ACTION
	Too Many Runs	This is when data points are continuously crossing the median line back and forth – this feels similar to a flat distribution in a histogram – no clear pattern emerges.	Think about other ways to stratify or categorize your data. Are you looking at data that has been aggregated and could be disaggregated to assess for patterns?
	Bias: at least 14 points in a row alternating up and down	This is an interesting pattern that typically emerges when data has been made up. Our brains try to make up "random" data but instead we end up producing something that looks like this.	Just because your data looks like this doesn't mean it is fake data – but check the source and validate it before moving on. If the data is accurate, then see if there is an explanation for the pattern or stratify the data differently.

We can tell a lot about a process by looking at the patterns that emerge in a run chart, but we can also add a greater element of statistical rigor by using a control chart instead of a run chart. Control charts have mathematical principles that help us to better understand the variation in a data set. We've talked about variation occurring in our data sets several times now, but let's take a closer look at the concept. Variation simply refers to the changes in a process that occur during a given time period. Variation exists in everything that we do in healthcare. Nothing about healthcare is the same as making widgets. We don't set machines to a specific setting and then watch each widget come out the same. In healthcare there are a number of factors (called variables) that contribute to how a process performs.

There is variation in the length of an exam (no doctor turns out every patient at exactly 30 minutes, regardless of how the schedule is set up), infection rates, wait times in the emergency department, inpatient length of stay, and just about any other metric in healthcare that you can think of. These are processes that involve humans, and humans come with a whole host of variables!

We can't make variation in a process disappear, but we can work to improve our processes so that they contain less variation. Variation in a process leads to unpredictability. If daily appointment volumes fluctuate between 50 and 150 on any given day, it would be really difficult to staff that clinic appropriately. Some days we would be overstaffed and other days we would be understaffed. In addition, if wait time varies from five minutes to an hour and five minutes, patients don't know what to expect when they arrive, which can make them more dissatisfied than if they know you will consistently be twenty minutes late.

Control charts are really helpful for looking at the data and understanding our variation by classifying it as either common cause or special cause variation. In order to improve a process and reduce variation, you need to know which type of variation you are dealing with because the reaction to each should be different.

TYPE OF VARIATION	DEFINITION	EXAMPLES	SUGGESTED REACTION
Common Cause	Variation that occurs due to natural fluctuations in the system; stable and predictable	• Patient discharge times from unit to unit • Temperature changes in the OR during the day • EMR startup time upon opening the application	• Review the data set as a whole to gain a comprehensive understanding of the system • Make changes to the process as a whole for improvement • Do not spend time isolating the differences between individual data points and possibly overreacting to the variation
Special Cause	Variation that occurs from a specific cause not inherent in the system; assignable	• High usage of Personal Protective Equipment (PPE) supplies during a cDiff outbreak • ED volumes during Motorcycle Week • Lab turnaround time after installation of a new instrument	• Understand what is different between the individual data points. • Is there a known or discernable reason for the special cause? • Take action based on the reported difference to reduce the occurrence of special cause • If special cause is unavoidable (cancellations due to snow storms) – then the focus should be on the plan for handling special cause situations when they arise

A control chart performs all of the same functions as a run chart, but also helps to identify signs of special cause variation. These signs of special cause come from statisticians who have isolated patterns that are not likely to occur due to random chance. If they occur, there is typically a reason, or a special cause, for why they have occurred. Control charts and the rules for special cause associated with them are derived from principles related to normal data and the empirical rule. Although you do not have to have normal data to use a control chart, understanding principles of normal data can help you to understand how control limits are calculated. On a control chart, the center line is the mean (not the median like in a run chart) and there are two control limits (upper and lower) that are calculated based on the mean. Depending on the type of control chart used, the calculations are slightly different but they all are based on an approximation of three standard deviations from the mean. If you think back to the empirical rule (that really cool rule associated with normal data), then you might remember that there is a less than 1% chance that a data point will fall farther than three standard deviations from the mean. This is why in a control chart, one signal for special cause is a data point that falls outside of the control limits. Let's look at the tool first, and then review signs of special cause.

Tool: Control Chart

PURPOSE: A control chart operates in a similar manner to a run chart, allowing for the identification of trends and patterns within time-ordered data. A control chart also has the added element of including upper and lower control limits as well as the process mean. These additional elements of the graph make it easier to understand if a process is stable or if there are instances of special cause variation that might need to be addressed.

HOW TO COMPLETE:

1. Using Microsoft Excel, with the SPC XL add-in enabled, set up the data in two columns. If the data is already in a workbook in two columns (time period in one and variable data in the other), this can be done from the original workbook.

2. Click on the "SigmaZone" tab at the top, select the "Control Charts" dropdown menu, then choose "Indiv MovR Chart" (or the most appropriate chart for your data set, see table after the example).

3. A box will pop up asking for the data range and the X-Axis labels. Select the appropriate data range – this should be all of the values for the measurement. Then select the appropriate X-Axis Labels – this should be the time labels (month, week, etc.). Click "Next". Do not select any titles or headers with these ranges; this will create an error.

4. Another pop-up box will give the option to also create a histogram of the selected data. If this is desired, check the appropriate boxes and click "Next" or "Finish".

Tips:

- In order for a control chart to show meaningful control limits, the chart should have at least 24 data points.

- The data should be set up in time order from earliest to latest.

- SPC XL will automatically highlight out-of-control points as red. In order to change the default rules click on the "SigmaZone" tab, "Options", and then "Out of Control". Here the rules for defining an out of control point can be adjusted.

- If there is a process shift, it is often helpful to calculate new control limits. This can still be done on one control chart by adding a split in the control limits. Click on the control chart, select the "SigmaZone" tab and choose "Split Control Limits". A box will pop up with a list of X-axis values. Select where the split (or splits) should occur and move those values into the right hand column box. Select "OK". (We will talk about the need for this in Control.)

- Although a control chart may or may not be used during the Measure phase of a project, it can still be used during the Control phase to assess changes in the process and to continue to monitor performance over time.

- Control charts are available in many statistical programs. Review your program to learn how to set up data to construct a control chart.

Example:
Ophthalmology Clinic Flow

The control chart below looks at the total patient wait time during a Retina visit in clinic. Each data point is the wait time average for a week. In the chart that we can see there is one data point that falls outside of the control limits, indicating that something specific might have occurred that week to make wait times longer than the other weeks plotted here. The second chart is showing the moving range. This means that each dot is indicating the difference between the two data points in the top chart.

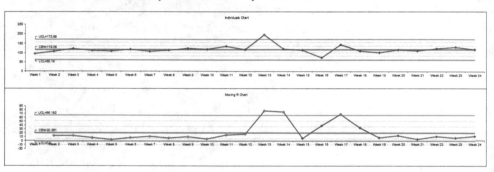

There are many different types of control charts, and choosing the correct one can be a challenge. SPC XL has a wizard tool that will help you select the correct one, other statistical packages often have something similar. You can utilize the following charts to choose the correct type of control chart. First identify if you have continuous or discrete data, and then review the charts to make the appropriate selection. When in doubt, use the IMR chart, as it is the least sensitive chart and will be less likely to give you false signs of special cause when used with data other than its intended use.

CONTROL CHARTS FOR CONTINUOUS DATA		
CHART TYPE	**WHEN IT IS USED**	**EXAMPLES**
X-bar and R	When you are measuring subgroups (samples); when there are 10 or less data points per sample *Note the range is used to set control limits due to the small sample size*	Length of appointment time per day (less than 10 data points per day) ED wait time per hour (less than 10 data points per hour)
X-bar and S	When you are measuring subgroups (samples); when there are more than 10 data points per sample	ED wait time per day (more than 10 data points per day) Length of appointment time per day (more than 10 data points per day)
Individuals Moving Range (IMR)	Used when measuring the full process or population (no sampling) This is the default chart to use when unsure of data types and details	Length of appointment time per day (when all appointments for the day are included) ED wait time by month (when all ED visits are included)

CONTROL CHARTS FOR DISCRETE DATA		
CHART TYPE	**WHEN IT IS USED**	**EXAMPLES**
u-chart	Used with a variable sample size (the number of samples collected each day might be inconsistent) There are multiple opportunities for defects per unit	# of coding errors per the monthly total of appointments # of medication errors per total patient census each day
p-chart	Used with a variable sample size (the number of samples collected each day might be inconsistent) There is only one opportunity for a defect per unit (the unit is considered defective or acceptable) Chart is created as a percentage (percent defective of the total)	% of surgery cases that started late per day % of triage calls not resolved on the 1st point of contact per week
c-chart	Used when the sample size is constant There are multiple opportunities for defects per unit	# of errors in inpatient dietary trays per 20 observations per week # of coding errors per 20 chart reviews per month
np-chart	Used when the sample size is constant There is only one opportunity for a defect per unit (the unit is considered defective or acceptable)	# of patient encounters without hand hygiene per 30 observations per day # of late patient arrivals per 20 observations per day

In addition to understanding signs of special cause, the control chart also helps to indicate if the process as a whole is stable or unstable. A stable process is predictable and lends itself well to process improvement work. It contains mostly common cause variation. An unstable process is unpredictable, often needs to be stabilized before it can be improved, and is indicated by frequent signs of special cause. A stable process may or may not be meeting customer specifications. If you have a stable process that is not meeting expectations, you might want to make fundamental process changes. Whereas, if you have a stable process that is meeting customer expectations, you can work to focus on those rare instances of special cause. Sometimes when special cause is present, that doesn't necessarily mean that a process is unstable. For example, as healthcare employees in the northeast, we often see data that looks funky in the winter months. If we are looking at appointment volumes or no-show rates for our clinics, we can often associate funny data points with snowstorms. Yes, the process has special cause variation, but that doesn't make the process unstable, because we know that this is just a fact of life in the northeast. Let's look at a chart to better understand signs of special cause (these will look similar to run chart patterns, but note that these have mathematical support for being special cause). The rules for both control charts and run charts will sometimes vary depending on the source, but have all been adapted from Dr. Walter Shewhart's statistical process control (SPC) principles.

VISUAL EXAMPLE OF SHAPE	NAME/ DESCRIPTION	CONCLUSION	ACTION
	Trend: at least 8 points in a row, increasing or decreasing	Something in the process likely changed at the start of the trend.	Determine if this is a good trend or a bad trend. Investigate the point in time when the trend started and try to determine its cause.
	Shift: at least 7 points in a row, above or below the mean	Something in the process likely changed at the start of the shift.	Determine if this is a good shift or a bad shift. Investigate the point in time when the shift occurred and try to determine its cause.
	Bias: at least 14 points in a row alternating up and down	This is an interesting pattern that typically emerges when data has been made up. Our brains try to make up "random" data but instead we end up producing something that looks like this.	Just because your data looks like this doesn't mean it is fake data – but check the source and validate it before moving on. If the data is accurate – then see if there is an explanation for the pattern or stratify the data differently.

VISUAL EXAMPLE OF SHAPE	NAME/ DESCRIPTION	CONCLUSION	ACTION
	Zone A: 2 of 3 consecutive points beyond 2 standard deviations (on the same side)	These zone rules are most appropriate with normal data. If your data is not normal you might get a false signal of special cause. This is a signal of special cause because it is statistically unlikely to occur due to random chance.	Review the data points marked as special cause and determine if there is a process explanation. Makes changes to prevent future occurrence of this special cause or implement mitigation strategies if it cannot be avoided.
	Zone B: 4 of 5 consecutive points beyond 1 standard deviation (on the same side)	These zone rules are most appropriate with normal data. If your data is not normal you might get a false signal of special cause. This is a signal of special cause because it is statistically unlikely to occur due to random chance.	Review the data points marked as special cause and determine if there is a process explanation. Make changes to prevent future occurrence of this special cause or implement mitigation strategies if it cannot be avoided.
	Zone C: 14 consecutive points within 1 standard deviation above or below the mean	These zone rules are most appropriate with normal data. If your data is not normal you might get a false signal of special cause. This is a signal of special cause because it is statistically unlikely to occur due to random chance.	Review the data points marked as special cause and determine if there is a process explanation. Make changes to prevent future occurrence of this special cause or implement mitigation strategies if it cannot be avoided.

VISUAL EXAMPLE OF SHAPE	NAME/ DESCRIPTION	CONCLUSION	ACTION
	Data point outside of control limits	Any time that a data point falls outside of the control limits, it is a sign of special cause. This is because control charts are based on the empirical rule, so there is (presumably) a less than 1% chance that a data point would fall outside of control limits due to random chance. There is likely an explanation.	Review the data point and determine if there is a process explanation. Make changes to prevent future occurrence of this special cause or implement mitigation strategies if it cannot be avoided.

At this point in Measure, you have collected and visualized data to better understand your process. It is important, not only to understand your process, but to see how your process is comparing in relation to customer specifications. Remember those measurable characteristics from your CTx tree? If you have those, or other performance specifications/targets, you can add those notes to your data visuals. This helps to see how often the process is performing to target. We encourage you to add specifications or targets to visuals as this can be a helpful way to talk to your team and your sponsor about the current state of the process.

Another way to think about our data is in terms of defects. We can capture data specifically designed to determine the number of defects in a process, or we can adjust our thinking about performance data. Any time that data falls outside of customer specifications, we could call that a defect. If I am reviewing the length of time that it takes to schedule an appointment and my customer specification is that all appointments should be scheduled within 14 days of the referral, I can take every instance that took longer than 14 days and count those as defects. If I am counting the number of CLABSIs (central line infections), each of those is in itself a defect, and I would also need to understand the number of total patients with central lines, to determine my rate of defects in the overall process.

Six Sigma is a term for understanding process capability based on the number of defects per million opportunities. Defects are when a customer specification is not met. Opportunities are the number of times that a defect could be created (not the ways in which they could occur). In the example above about patient infection we might say there are two opportunities for infection: upon installation of the central line and during maintenance of the central line. Now there are many different factors that could cause an infection at either point, but there are two opportunities for it to occur.

In order to understand defects per million opportunities (DPMO), we would do a calculation:

$$\frac{\text{Defects}}{\text{Opportunities X Units}} \quad X \quad \text{1 Million} \quad = \text{Defects Per Million Opportunities}$$

This calculation is part of a process capability assessment. It helps us to understand if our process is meeting customer specifications. So, this is something that you can look at with both a visual and mathematically. Six Sigma means that a process has 3.4 defects per million. Don't be alarmed if you complete this calculation and your process is performing nowhere near 3.4 defects per million, very few healthcare processes have reached that level of performance. The goal is to reduce your number of defects per million as a result of the improvement efforts.

VISUALIZE THE PROCESS

We've spent a lot of time talking about how to collect and understand data associated with your process. But there is another really important piece of understanding current state that should take place in the Measure phase, and that is mapping the process flow. By using a flowchart, you can capture the entire process from beginning to end visually. This is really important in understanding all of the details of a process, getting all team members on the same page about what happens in the process, and quickly identifying bottlenecks or redundancies in the current state of the work.

You can create a standard flowchart that shows the process in detail step-by-step, or you can use a swimlane flowchart. A swimlane flowchart captures the process in the same way, but adds in roles or departments so that it is clear who is responsible for each step in the process. The swimlane can be beneficial if there are many people involved in the process, ownership is a concern, or you suspect that there are a lot of handoffs from one role to another (handoffs in a process open up a chance for error to occur). The swimlane is helpful at making all of these things visual for the team to better understand and think about.

Before completing a flowchart with your team, it is important to observe the process firsthand. This helps in ensuring that you understand the process and have a frame of reference to capture the details. When observing, do not interrupt staff completing the work. You should really be a fly on the wall just observing the process and making notes. You should save questions for staff until later, but do introduce yourself to staff and patients if they ask why you are there. If you already did this while collecting data, then hopefully you have a clear enough picture to walk the team through a flowchart. If you haven't yet observed the process, then you should do that now. Seriously – NOW. Do not read any more of this until you observe the process; it really is one of the most valuable aspects of process improvement work.

Tool: Flowchart

PURPOSE: A flowchart is a detailed overview of an entire process that is used as a visual representation of the process from beginning to end. This allows the team to agree on the current state and highlight the process for those members who may not be familiar with all of the steps.

HOW TO COMPLETE:

1. Determine the start and end points of the process to be documented. (Refer back to project scope in the charter, if necessary.)

2. Walk through the process from start to finish thinking about each individual step. Use decision points for aspects of the process that might drive the rest of the process in two different directions (even if only temporarily before the two processes join again).

3. Put the steps in order from beginning to end.

4. Place the flowchart in an area where the work team responsible for the process can see it. They may have additional insight into the process to share.

Tips:

- Think about using sticky notes when creating a flowchart with the team. Doing this electronically can be very cumbersome. Sticky notes allow for steps to be easily moved and rearranged as additional steps are recalled. It can also help the team to feel more involved if they are helping to document the steps.

- If the team desires to make the flowchart electronic, this can be done in Microsoft Excel, PowerPoint, or Visio.

- Remember, there are two types of flowcharts.

  - Standard: This is the detailed map of the process, being sure to think about decision points and individual steps.

  - Swimlane Flowchart: This is a flowchart that groups the steps by the person (or group) responsible for doing them.

- Below are the most common flowchart shapes to get you started.

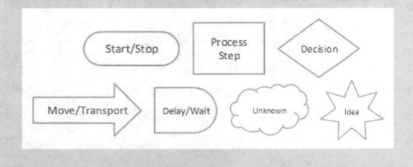

Example:

Pathway to Discharge

In the Pathway to Discharge process map, a standard flowchart was utilized to map the admission process with additional titles on the side to denote high level steps. This helped to illustrate where handoffs were occurring.

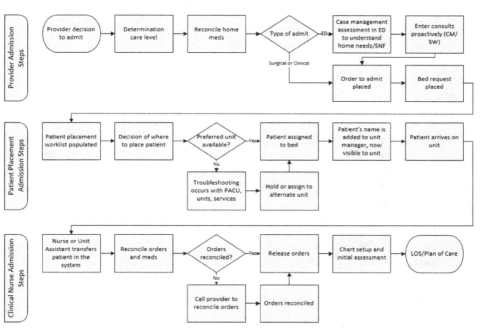

Once you have completed the flowchart, you should share it with staff outside of the immediate team who also work in the process. Hang it in a public area, or share a digital version if staff are dispersed. Allow staff to comment on the flowchart, add information, or ask questions. This can provide additional insight into the process and help to capture elements that may have been missed in the initial creation.

We have chosen to talk about the flowchart at the end of the

Measure chapter, so that all of the data information flows nicely from our discussion of the CTx tree. However, that does not mean that you need to wait until the end of the Measure phase to create your flowchart. In fact, the flowchart will often be created in a team meeting, while you are also in the process of collecting data, and that is okay! What is important is that by the end of Measure you have both data and a process map (flowchart) to help truly understand current state.

Once you have all of that completed, you are likely ready to move from the Measure phase to the Analyze phase. If you are closing out each phase of the project by meeting with your sponsor, then go ahead and schedule that next meeting. Here are some of the questions that you should ask yourself at the end of Measure and discuss with your sponsor:

- What is the baseline performance of the process?
- How are we performing against our performance targets?
- What new understanding did the team gain by mapping the process?
- Are there specific characteristics of the data that help us understand the problem better?
- Based on the current data, is the work worth continuing?

If you can answer these questions, then you're ready to move on to Analyze! Analyze is one of the best phases because you really start to learn about your process and think about the problem in new ways. I know we tricked you a little by telling you that Measure was fun, but we really just wanted you to read this chapter because it is so important! Analyze really is fun! You can trust us!

Chapter Four:
Analyze

The ultimate goal of Analyze is to determine the root causes of the problem to ensure that any solutions will address the appropriate sources of the problem. You can think about breaking Analyze down into three sections: perform lean analysis, identify potential causes, and verify root causes. This chapter will provide you with an overview of how to apply the primary Analyze tools to your project. In Analyze there are many options for tools to use. Note that not every tool will be utilized in each project, but we want to show you the variety of options available. Think of this as an *a la carte* menu. You can select the tools most appropriate for your project as long as you walk away understanding (and validating) the true root causes of your problem.

PERFORM LEAN ANALYSIS

Lean is such an important part of the Lean Six Sigma combo, and while we have mostly been talking about elements of Six Sigma thus far, we are going to devote a whole portion of this chapter to talking about Lean. We're going to do it again in Improve too! Lean has concepts and tools that can apply to most project work. For now, we will focus on some of the lean analysis concepts and tools, and in Improve we will talk about common Lean solutions (that can be applied based on these analyses).

Before we look at some of the tools, it is really important to understand some of the foundational principles of Lean thinking. Lean is so much more than a toolkit, it can really transform the way you look at your work. I'm sure that sounds exactly like what people who are too into their work would say. We know this. But it really is, and we'll just focus on trying to convince you that it's true. Lean focuses on maximizing value to the customer by identifying and eliminating waste in the process. By looking at a process from a customer's perspective, we can understand what value the process is providing. A key component of Lean is that we always do this while also showing respect for people who do the work. We need to value the knowledge and contribution that staff bring to any process. When we start throwing around words like "waste" and "value", it can start to make people question if we think their work is valuable. We need to be sensitive to this when performing a Lean analysis.

Let's take a look at the five principles of Lean thinking (Adapted from: Womack and Jones, 2003[1]):

Identify customer and specify value	In most processes (especially those in healthcare!), only a small fraction of the total time and effort in a process adds value to the customer. The goal is to identify which activities add value and which do not, and to target non-value activities (waste) for removal.
Identify and map value stream	A value stream looks at a process from end-to-end, looking at the entire set of activities across all parts of the organization that jointly provide a product or service. In healthcare, this could mean from the time the patient calls to schedule an appointment until they receive a bill for that care – we can review that entire process as one value stream that crosses several departments.

1 Womack, J.P., & Jones, D.T. (2003) Lean thinking: banish waste and create wealth in your corporation. Simon & Schuster, Inc. New York, NY.

Create flow by eliminating waste	An ideal process will flow smoothly without any interruptions, waiting, or other detours. This is most commonly achieved by eliminating waste and process bottlenecks.
Respond to customer pull	Processes should be set up to meet customer demand. This requires that we first understand what customer demand is. Once we know our demand, we can design the process to produce what the customer wants, when the customer wants it.
Pursue perfection	Although true perfection in a healthcare process is unrealistic (there are always too many factors to consider with people), the point is to keep aiming for perfection. Continue to make a process the best that it can be by removing waste and increasing value continuously.

Analyzing a process for waste is one of those things that gets a process improvement guru out of bed in the morning. It's also one of those things that drives members of their household insane from time to time. (Turns out people don't love being told that they're inefficient at a basic household task – but they get used to it!). There are several different categories of waste that can be present. In the chart below, you'll find eight wastes (that make up the acronym DOWNTIME), plus a couple of bonus types of waste (the original eight have been adapted from the Toyota Production System). Each of these has a definition and some healthcare examples that you've probably seen before.

TYPE OF WASTE	DEFINITION	HEALTHCARE EXAMPLES	HOME EXAMPLES (IN CASE YOU WANT TO PRACTICE DRIVING PEOPLE NUTS)
DEFECTS	A mistake or error in the service or product	• Patient contracting a hospital-acquired infection • Getting a needle stick while suturing	• A red sock turning all the white laundry pink • Breaking dishes when unloading the dishwasher
OVERPRODUCTION	Producing work prior to it being requested or needed by the customer (just in case, rather than just in time)	• Performing a test too far in advance of a procedure (it will likely need to be redone) • Compiling reports that no one is using	• Packing medication for all possible scenarios when going on vacation
WAITING	Waiting for supplies, equipment, information, or staff Important note about waiting: sometimes waiting is necessary in a process – if you can be doing something else that moves the process along instead of only waiting, that can help reduce the waste associated with the wait	• Patients waiting in the waiting room • Waiting for information to make a decision and move to the next step	• Waiting for your children to make their way to the car in the morning • Waiting for the oven to preheat
NON-UTILIZED TALENT	Staff not performing to the top of their license or scope of practice; not using people's skills from prior experience in their current work	• Lack of cross training • RN registering patients • Providers scheduling appointments	• A performance improvement guru not applying these skills at home • Children (of appropriate age) not putting their own dishes in the dishwasher

TYPE OF WASTE	DEFINITION	HEALTHCARE EXAMPLES	HOME EXAMPLES (IN CASE YOU WANT TO PRACTICE DRIVING PEOPLE NUTS)
TRANSPORTATION	Moving patients, supplies, or information farther than is necessary	• Uncoordinated testing resulting in patients being transported multiple times • Walking to the lab with a specimen instead of sending it in a tube system	• Walking upstairs to a coat closet instead of having coats located near the exit • Walking back and forth from the garage to the living room because you didn't get all tools needed for the project upfront
INVENTORY	Excess supplies, equipment, or materials that are not needed. This often results in expired products and costs money. This can also result in a lack of space for necessary items.	• Large quantities of medicine that are infrequently used • Keeping obsolete equipment when it's been replaced	• Keeping old tablets after upgrading to the new iPad • Buying groceries in bulk that expire before the family can consume them
MOTION	Movement that requires us to move in ways that might damage the body. The focus here is on ergonomics and optimal space configuration.	• Receptionists getting up constantly to retrieve a medication list from the printer • Repetitive bending and reaching for frequently used items that are stored too high or low	• Having your most frequently used dishes on the top shelf • Keeping commonly used food in the basement freezer

TYPE OF WASTE	DEFINITION	HEALTHCARE EXAMPLES	HOME EXAMPLES (IN CASE YOU WANT TO PRACTICE DRIVING PEOPLE NUTS)
EXCESS PROCESSING	Producing or processing to a higher standard than is required by the customer	• Ordering a CT when an ultrasound would provide the information necessary • An after-visit summary that is written with terminology that is unfamiliar to the patient	• Cooking a really fancy dinner when your family just wants tacos • Buying top-of-the-line bottled water when the store brand would be fine • Making a dessert when the family is already full from dinner
BONUS WASTES!			
UNEVENNESS	Pace of the work is not consistent. There are peaks and dips in demand than can cause work to be rushed and then lag. Process irregularities might exist due to inconsistent practices.	• Overbooking appointments • Inconsistent inventory levels • Huge differences in patient panel numbers	• Skipping the dishes one night, then they pile up and the next night they don't all fit in the dishwasher, then you spend twice as long on dishes the next two days, making up for the one skipped day (this is most definitely not a real-life scenario that we have experienced)
OVERBURDEN	Inducing unnecessary stress on people or equipment. Working harder, longer, or with greater effort than is reasonable	• Signs in people: errors, decrease in quality, turnover, lower priority tasks never get completed • Signs in equipment: breakdowns, no preventative maintenance is performed, used well past its useful life	• Do we even need to explain this one? We all experience this when we overextend ourselves!

Once we understand the types of waste that might be present in a process, we can identify when that waste is occurring. Then, you have the opportunity to remove that waste as part of the Improve phase. Additionally, identifying and removing waste is something that you can do in a process even if you aren't doing a full-scale project. If we see our staff doing rework, we address it and see if there are opportunities to avoid this. The trick is just to make sure that you understand the full scope of the work happening before making large changes. Minor tweaks to remove waste are usually okay. And that is precisely what makes Lean thinking so critical! If you can go back and look at your work through a Lean lens that targets waste, you can make large differences with minimal effort.

Let's shift our focus from waste to the concept of a value stream. As we mentioned above, a value stream is an end-to-end process that produces a product or service. You can look at components of value streams or entire value streams. For example, if a patient arrives in the emergency department, the value stream might be from arrival until discharge, or it might be from arrival to bill paid. How you define the value stream, depends on your area of focus.

In order to understand how a value stream is operating, you can use a tool called a Value Stream Map. This is another type of process map that looks at process steps (typically higher level than the flowchart), but also adds data and information to paint a full picture. You can include information such as resources, process time, and wait time to understand each component of the value stream.

Tool: Value Steam Map

PURPOSE: To illustrate the flow of material and information as a product or service makes its way through a value stream.

HOW TO COMPLETE:

1. In order to complete a Value Stream Map, you must first observe the process and understand what is happening first-hand. Be sure to pay attention to the key steps of the process as well as any waste or general observations worth noting.

2. Next, determine the data that should be collected about the process. This might be the time that it takes for each process step, the resources available for each process step, or information about defects noticed in the process.

3. Utilizing a data collection form, go watch the work being done and collect data. Alternatively, an electronic report can be used to gather the data as long as you have already observed and have a solid understanding of the data needed. Translate data into the necessary format for constructing the value stream map.

4. Next, document the process flow in a linear flowchart. These will likely be high-level process steps. They might even align with your SIPOC steps.

5. Add information flows that are relevant to the process.

6. Next, add the time ladder and indicate the time associated with each process step and the time between steps.

7. Add any other resources or additional information that is relevant.

Tips:

- A value stream map can seem busy or over-whelming at first glance. Start by mapping the process flow before trying to add the other components. Thinking about this one step at a time can make the task much more reasonable.

- Every value stream map will look different. The information included on one value stream map might not be necessary on another. Don't get too caught up in one or two value stream map styles. Experiment and utilize the information that is necessary to understand your process.

- Below are common value stream map shapes

	Process Step		Customer/Suppliers
	Information Flow		Information Recipient
	Transition to next step (no movement)		Material/People Movement
	Observation Required		Delay
	Queue • Avg: Average Count in Queue • Min: Minimum Count in Queue • Max: Maximum Count in Queue		Data Box • PT: Process Time (Minutes) • Min: Minimum PT (Minutes) • Min: Maximum PT (Minutes) • RES: Resources (Staff)
	Time Ladder		

Review the chart below for a list of common data points you can include in a value stream map, their abbreviations, and definitions.

DATA POINT	ABBR.	DEFINITION
Process time	PT	Time the person or product is acted on to get closer to the end goal
Wait time	WT	Time where a product or patient is waiting to take the next action (between process steps)
Cycle time	CT	The total time from the beginning to the end of your process. Cycle time includes process time and wait time
Count in queue	Q	Count of things (people, equipment, supplies, product, etc.) waiting for next step
Total lead time	TLT	The total time (Value Add and Non-Value Add) it takes a product to make it through the entire value stream
% Complete & Accurate	% CA	% of time the step receives information that is complete and accurate
Minimum	Min	Minimum amount (count or time)
Maximum	Max	Maximum amount (count or time)
Time in queue	Q	Amount of time things are waiting (use a different abbreviation if also using count in queue)
Frequency %		How often a particular situation happens as a percent of the total number
Resources	R	The people or equipment utilized to perform the process duties or tasks
Customer Demand		The quantity of a product or service required by the customer for a given period of time

DATA POINT	ABBR.	DEFINITION
TAKT time	TAKT	The required pace of work in order to meet demand, Takt Time = Time Available/Demand (more about this in a few pages)
Change-over time	CO	The time to change over or set-up a room, patient, paperwork, machine, or program etc. (from the end of the last cycle to the beginning of the next cycle)
Right first time %	RFT	Sometimes called First Pass Yield; percentage units that meet all quality standards, percent of units/patients done correctly
First in first out	FIFO	Activity is performed in the order it enters the process step
Information technology		Systems, software, databases used. Identify communication points
Number of iterations		Count of attempts to complete the step or activity
Batch sizes		When batching is part of a process, how much or how often the work is performed
Customer satisfaction data		Data that measures satisfaction of customers/ patients of the value stream. Useful for understanding customer specifications

Example:
Ophthalmology Clinic Flow

The value stream map below shows the high-level flow of the Ophthalmology clinic with wait times and process times calculated for each step. There is no time listed between the provider exam and check-out because patients were able to check out with a secretary after their visit without having to wait. This data may look different from some of the data in the Measure section as the value stream map was created from observation data only. We created the value stream map before we worked out the kinks in getting consistent data from the EMR.

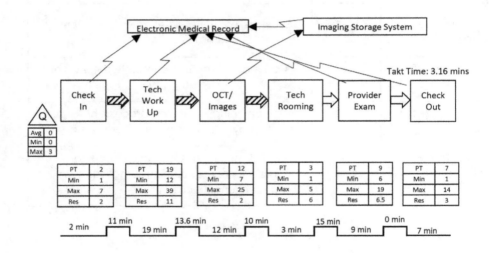

Whether or not you decide that a value stream map is necessary for your project, you can still do another type of Lean analysis called value added analysis. A value added analysis is when you look at each step in the process and determine if it is adding value to the customer, waste, or a business non-value added step. Review the definitions below and then see how to complete this analysis on a flowchart or value stream map. A value added analysis should always be done from the customer's perspective. What does the customer think is valuable? You might ask yourself "Would the customer pay more for this step?" to help determine if a step is valuable. Additionally, you might consult voice of the customer comments to see if that provides insight into what the customer finds valuable.

Value Added	Process time that improves or changes the form, fit, or function of a patient, product, or service
Non-Value Added	Wait time or process time that adds no value to the patient, product or process from a customer's perspective (i.e. waiting, inspection, rework). This is true waste that we learned about with the DOWNTIME acronym.
Business Non-Value Added	Process time that is required for business operations but adds no value to the customer. In healthcare, sometimes regulatory or compliance activities may fall into this category.
Process Efficiency	Value added process time as a percentage of cycle time VA PT/CT = Process Efficiency (%)

Tool: Value Added Analysis

PURPOSE: To look at the current state process and assess each process step to determine whether or not it adds value to the customer experience.

HOW TO COMPLETE:

1. Use a flowchart of the current process or a value stream map conducted by the team to start the value added analysis.

2. Look at each process step and determine if that step is value added, non-value added, or business non-value added.

3. Use the tips below to think about waste in the process and to help assess value added steps from the customer perspective.

4. Choose colored markers and go through marking each step with the appropriate category, or crossing out the non-value added steps.

5. If you have the process time for each of the process steps, it is also possible to calculate process efficiency. This is the value added process time as a percentage of cycle time.

    a. Value Added Process Time/Total Cycle Time = Process Efficiency (%)

Tips:

- While business non-value added process steps might be necessary to the process flow, that does not mean that they can't also be optimized and improved. A business non-value added process step might still be able to take less time when optimized properly

  - For business non-value added time, be sure to ask why this step has to be completed. Is it truly essential to the business? Is there a way to optimize the time spent on this step? For example, if patients in a clinic are receiving a survey at the end of their visit and they are upset about the time it takes, this could be considered a business non-value added step, but the process could also be modified so that the survey is mailed and patients don't have to stay in the clinic longer to complete it.

- Remember that value added analysis is always done from the customer's perspective. However, that does not always mean the patient in health-care. Many healthcare processes and systems have other customers of a process, particularly when serving an internal function.

- When doing a value added analysis, be sure to think about the staff perspective and ensure that you are showing respect for staff who do the work. Staff sometimes have a hard time if a step that they do is categorized as "non-value added". Talk through this with them to explain why the team is classifying it that way and help them to understand that it does not mean that their work isn't valuable. Healthcare workers in all areas often feel like their work is very valu-able and can struggle with this activity.

Example:
Ophthalmology Clinic Flow

While the value stream map alone was helpful in understanding process flow and times associated with the typical clinic visit in Ophthalmology, doing a value added analysis allowed the team to visualize how much of the process was value added for the patient. The green shading indicates a process step that was value added. The team agreed that check-in and check-out were both business non-value added and all of the wait time between steps was waste. The calculated process efficiency was 42.3%, indicating that less than half the time the patient spent in the clinic was viewed as value added.

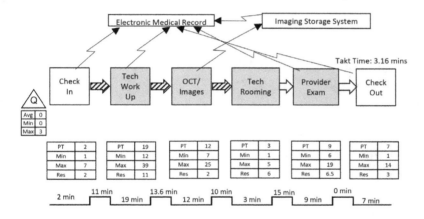

Value Added Process Time	43
Total Cycle Time	101.6
% Process Efficency	42.30%

Another great (and super easy) Lean analysis tool is a spaghetti diagram. A spaghetti diagram can be used to look at transportation or motion involved in a process. This is particularly useful if it seems like staff are moving all over the clinic to perform simple tasks (the clinic rooms are at one end, the waiting room is at another, the cleaning supplies are far away, the instruments needed for the patient exam are stored in a closet down the hall, etc.).

Tool: Spaghetti Diagram

PURPOSE: To create a visual representation of the motion, movement, or transportation of a person or item within a process to identify flow issues in workspace layout.

HOW TO COMPLETE:

1. Create or obtain a floorplan layout of the space where the work is done.

2. Go to the work location and observe.

3. Draw lines onto the map for each movement.

4. Use different colors for different activities, roles, or items (create a legend to keep track).

5. Make notes about areas where you might want to collect additional data.

Tips:

- Like with any observation, try not to interfere with the work. Ask questions as time allows or save for later.

- Complete proper planning before going to observe.

  - Will you be observing the patients? Employees? Or equipment flow?

  - Do you need to observe the process at different times?

  - Have you communicated to people that you will be observing and why?

  - Do you have the materials necessary to complete the drawing?

- This tool can be very useful when thinking about supply flow or organization, patient flow initiatives, or designing/optimizing an office or facility layout.

Example:
Ophthalmology Clinic Flow

This drawing outlines two different patient experiences. The patients who stay at the main clinic but move from hallway to hallway during the visit (blue) and patients who are transferred to the secondary clinic location, and have to walk back and forth to the main clinic for additional testing during their visit (green).

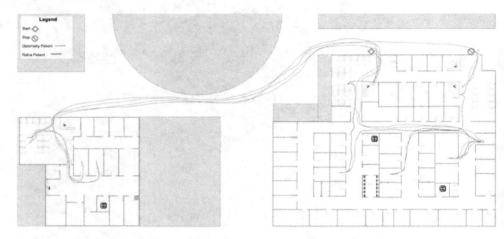

A more complex, but equally useful tool, is called workload analysis. Workload analysis is a tool that helps to review the balance of work between roles or steps in a process. Completing a workload analysis helps to highlight bottlenecks in a process by taking into account both time and resources available to meet demand. In order to perform a workload analysis, you first need to calculate something called Takt time.

Takt is a German word that means pace. Takt time, in Lean, refers to the pace of work required in order to meet customer demand. To calculate takt time, you divide working time available by customer demand. This tells you the pace at which the work needs to be done in order to meet the demand. This is a concept that works well in manufacturing. If the takt time is 5 minutes, you can interpret that as a product must come off the line every 5 minutes. In healthcare, this is a more abstract idea. We can say that a patient should be exiting the clinic every 5 minutes when looking at patient flow, but we know that a patient doesn't complete his/her entire visit in 5 minutes. Therefore, the takt time is more of a flow concept. We can compare the time of each process step against the calculated takt time to determine if the process is capable of maintaining the flow necessary to achieve takt time (and thus avoid bottlenecks and waiting for the patient).

A helpful example to consider is a public flu clinic. If a clinic is open for 3 hours a day (that is their capacity), and they typically have 80 patients coming to the clinic each day (that is their demand), we can calculate their takt time by first converting the hours to minutes; 180 minutes. Then we divide the capacity (number of available minutes) by the demand (number of patients). 180/80 = 2.25 minutes. This means that to meet demand, we need to have a patient leaving the flu clinic every 2.25 minutes. We can use this as an indicator of how many staff to hire. If it takes 4.5 minutes to administer a shot, we would need two people working the clinic. This is because we take the total process time and divide it by the number of resources. If the process time divided by the number of resources is greater than takt time, we can expect a bottleneck at that process step.

Tool: Workload Analysis

PURPOSE: To understand how the current process is performing in comparison to takt time. By limiting over-production or underproduction, the system can be stabilized to prevent build-ups of inventory and subsequent starts and stops.

HOW TO COMPLETE:

1. Setup an Excel spreadsheet that looks like the one below:

Role	Process Time (minutes)	Number of Resources	Per Person Process time	Takt Time	Additional Notes
Role 1					
Role 2					
Role 3					
Role 4					

2. First, list the roles or process steps (ex: Check-in Secretary, Nurse, Surgeon, Anesthesiologist).

3. Enter the process time (typically an average or median value) for each role or task.

4. Enter the number of resources available for each step or role (i.e. If there are two check-in staff, list 2. If there are four surgeons, list 4).

5. Create a formula in the per person process time column to calculate the total process time/the number of resources.

6. In the next column, list the calculated takt time for the process (available time/demand).

7. The final column can be used for any contextual notes.

8. Lastly, create a combination bar/line graph in Excel that will show each process step as a bar and the takt time as a line. Then you can compare each bar (process step) to the takt time line to understand current performance.

Tips:

- Takt time steps:
  a. Calculate demand: what does the end user or customer typically want every day/week/month
  b. Calculate available time: excluding breaks, meeting times
  c. Calculate Takt Time (available time/demand)
  d. Compare the actual process time against takt time using a chart
- Producing faster than Takt time results in overproduction
- Producing slower than Takt time results in bottlenecks or waiting

Example:
Ophthalmology Clinic Flow

In the Ophthalmology project, the team completed a workload analysis chart to understand each process step in the clinic flow. Based on the number of patients seen in clinic each day, the calculated takt time was just over three minutes. The workload analysis chart showed that a bottleneck was occurring at the imaging step (this is also where we observed patients waiting the longest during our observations in the clinic). This chart helped justify the need for better balancing resources to support this step.

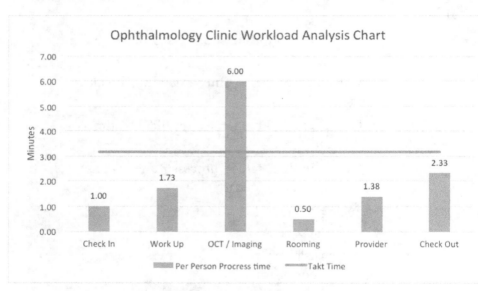

A final Lean concept to address at this point is the gemba walk. Gemba is a Japanese word that means "where the work is done". A gemba walk is simply going to where the work is done, with a purpose and goal to identify improvement opportunities. We don't have to tell you how important it is to go observe a process – because we told you in Measure and you could sense how important we feel this is. But just in case you missed it – let us remind you – YOU

MUST OBSERVE A PROCESS TO UNDERSTAND IT! Doing a gemba walk is an opportunity for you to observe the process, talk to the staff (without interfering), and understand how the work is done. This is great to do as part of the analysis during your project, but is also considered a best practice among managers and other leaders working in an organization that has embraced a Lean culture. Remember, as with any Lean activity, always do this respectfully.

IDENTIFY POTENTIAL CAUSES

This next phase of Analyze is critical because you want to ensure that your team is working to address the root causes of your problem and not just the symptoms. Imagine trying to get rid of the dandelions in your garden by simply cutting the dandelion at the base of the stem. What is the result? No surprises here, the dandelions grow right back because you didn't pull out the roots. Treating only the symptoms of a problem can result in wasted time, effort, and energy on the implementation of a solution that does not have the desired impact on your problem.

The process mapping and data collection you completed in the Measure phase provides a good base for initiating the work in Analyze. Additionally, the voice of customer information captured in Define can also serve as an excellent input to your team's discussion of potential root causes. The Lean analysis tools discussed above can also help you uncover root causes.

You may choose to utilize one or both of the tools in this section, but all projects should use at least one of these tools to identify potential root causes for your problem. In addition, you can utilize them together by completing the cause and effect diagram first and then applying the 5-whys technique to some of the causes identified in the diagram.

Tool: Cause and Effect Diagram (Fishbone)

PURPOSE: A cause and effect diagram is a tool designed to help understand the potential root causes for a focused problem statement. This tool helps the team to understand possible relationships between the problem and the potential root causes. It is particularly useful when there may be a larger number of contributing factors to the problem statement. The Cause and Effect Diagram may also be referred to as a Fishbone Diagram (because it looks like a fish) or the Ishikawa diagram (named after the developer of the tool, Kaoru Ishikawa who was a Japanese organizational theorist and professor).

HOW TO COMPLETE:

1. Start by coming up with a narrowly defined problem statement. This statement should be one that is agreed on by the team and written at the head of the "fish".

2. Next, determine the categories that should be used as bones of the "fish" (see tips for some examples). Most cause and effect diagrams have six bones; however, anywhere between four and eight is generally acceptable.

3. Finally, work with the team to brainstorm aspects of each category that might be contributing to the overall problem. Whenever possible, try to drill down even further using the 5 whys technique. For example, if one factor is that MAs are not rooming patients on time, ask "why". Thinking about that next level may help your team come up with other contributing factors such as "the patients are not in the waiting room when the MA goes to get them".

Tips:

- The cause and effect diagram is an activity that should be done by hand (not electronically) when working with the team. Sticky notes, whiteboards, or large posters can all work well for facilitating this activity.

- While facilitating this activity, it may be necessary to refocus the team at times and keep them on track. Remember to stay focused on the problem statement written at the head of the fish. In some circumstances a second diagram may be needed to address another problem statement related to the project, but stay as focused as possible on the one written down.

- Common cause and effect categories in healthcare are: people (can be broken down by role if necessary), materials, policies/procedures, measurement, environment, and equipment. Other categories can be used if they are more applicable to the problem being analyzed.

- When facilitating, redirect the team to the task at hand if they start trying to jump to solutions. Consider utilizing a "Parking Lot" poster on the wall to capture off topic discussion for future reference.

Example:
Pathway to Discharge

The Pathway to Discharge team had a robust discussion about the potential root causes for late discharges in the surgical nursing units. The team used the cause and effect diagram to determine where to focus their effort and energy. They selected four potential root causes including: visibility of discharge planning information in the EMR, pre-op patient education, variation in provider rounding structure and timing, and role clarity for all care team members regarding the components of the discharge process.

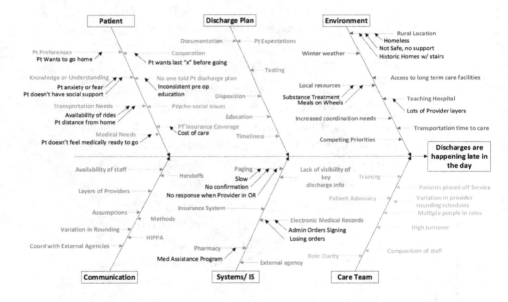

Tool: 5 Whys

PURPOSE: To dive deep into the root cause or sources of a problem by continuing to think about the next layer of "why" something is happening.

HOW TO COMPLETE:

1. Start by coming up with a narrowly defined problem statement. This statement should be one that is agreed on by the team and written on poster paper or a whiteboard.

2. Think about the problem statement and ask "why" this is happening.

3. Once the team gives a reason (or a few), continue with this process. Now ask "why" for each of those potential explanations.

4. Continue until it is not logical to ask "why" any further.

Tips:

- Focus on asking "why" and not "who". It can be natural for team members to give an answer of "Nurse A doesn't do her job properly" or "The managers don't take the time to do X activity". Focus on why this is occurring. What about the system makes it so that nurses don't get to a specific activity? Really focus on not blaming one individual or a group of individuals.

- Try to stay away from root causes that zero in on staffing concerns. While that may be a potential root cause for some issues, it is also unlikely to be something that is zeroed in on for improvement. Think about the resources available and the current system. Rather than "we are down a secretary" as the answer, perhaps the answer is "workload was not redistributed after a secretary left". This provides opportunity to try and work with the resources available to meet the overall need.

- 5 Whys is a general rule of thumb – it might be necessary to ask "why" fewer than five times or more than five times.

- To validate the 5 Whys response it can be useful to apply the "therefore" test. Start with the identified potential root cause and work backwards up the diagram – "(statement) therefore (statement above)". For example: "MAs have too many tasks assigned to them, therefore they are being pulled in too many directions"

  - If the "therefore" test doesn't seem to make a lot of sense – there might be a logical fallacy in the 5 Whys diagram. Go back and see if there is another potential "why" that would make more sense logically.

- It is normal for the 5 Whys diagram to branch out in different directions. Sometimes there are multiple reasons why something is happening. This is why there will typically be multiple possible root causes at the end of the activity.

Example:
Pathway to Discharge

The Pathway to discharge project team utilized the 5 Whys tool at the beginning of their work in the Analyze phase. The group started by asking why discharges are happening so late in the day. The first 5 Whys discussion focused on availability of testing results to make a discharge decision.

When utilizing the 5 Whys technique, the group quickly realized that they had numerous potential root causes to walk through, and switched over to facilitating the conversation utilizing the cause and effect diagram to capture the breadth and depth of the potential root causes for this project. They continued to utilize the 5 Whys conversational technique while working within the cause and effect diagram.

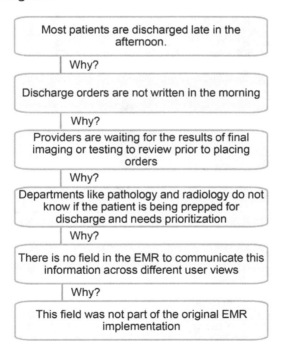

Example:
Ophthalmology Clinic Flow

The Ophthalmology team used the 5 Whys technique to address a handful of questions. Below is the 5 Whys analysis for understanding why there was no standard technician work-up. You can see that this example has branching as there was sometimes more than one answer to a question.

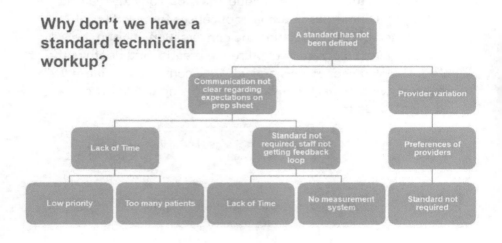

After you have worked with the team to determine the potential root causes, you then need to verify with (you guessed it!) data to ensure that they are actually contributing to your problem. You probably came up with many possible causes, and it just isn't feasible to verify all of them. So, the first step is to narrow down the list.

Consider the following factors when determining which potential root causes to verify:

- What are the most likely contributors to the problem?

- How measurable are each of the likely contributors?
- Which potential causes would you be able to take action on? If something is not in your control (such as a requirement for insurance purposes), it probably doesn't make sense to move forward with that cause.

A great technique for the team to use at this point is called multivoting. Multivoting is popular among project teams because it is quick, easy, and solicits input from all team members. To multivote with your team, simply list all of the potential causes (if you did a cause and effect diagram you can just use that!). Ensure clarity around all listed items and combine like items with team agreement. Give each team member the same number of votes (we usually like to give 10) and have them vote on the causes that they believe have the most impact on the problem and are within the scope of the project to address. Tally the votes and then move forward to verification with the top causes. As a team you will need to decide how many to verify based on bandwidth and importance. Votes can be placed on the cause and effect diagram or listed by using hash marks or (way more fun) stickers!

VERIFY ROOT CAUSES

Once you have narrowed down your list of potential root causes, you are ready to verify the remaining causes. Verification of root causes is an important step in the Analyze phase. Although you used all of the knowledge that you've gained about your problem to generate a list of possible causes, you need to make sure that there is data to back up those perceived connections. In some instances, you might have already collected the data necessary to verify your root causes in the Measure phase, but sometimes you might need to get additional data at this stage.

We recommend creating a plan to keep track of potential root causes and to determine which verification tools to utilize. Having a plan for verifying your potential root causes will allow you to generate a summary of the thinking process that begins with identifying potential root causes and ends with a set of verified root causes (sometimes called critical Xs) that have been established through appropriate testing and evaluation. Your plan can be super simple – no need for frills here. Take a look at the suggestion below.

POTENTIAL ROOT CAUSE	VERIFICATION TOOL	VERIFIED? (Y/N)

When verifying root causes, the first step is to develop a hypothesis for each potential root cause. A hypothesis is a suggested explanation of an occurrence or a prediction about a causal relationship between two factors. A hypothesis is usually generated from a belief that two factors are interrelated, whether or not there is initial data to support that belief. The hypothesis can then be tested to determine if there is evidence to support a relationship. Your hypothesis is that (insert potential root cause) is causing (insert problem). It might sound like a fancy science word (and be giving you flashbacks to elementary school) – but you totally have this!

Once you have your hypotheses and your plan ready to go, you can start to think about which tools will work best for the potential causes that you are working with. There is a whole toolkit available to you for this. Remember that while tools are recommended for certain phases of DMAIC, they should be used wherever they make the most sense.

When thinking about which tools to use, your focus should be on the degree of certainty needed to claim a causal relationship and what data you have available. For those of you with a research background, this can sometimes be the tricky part of process improvement work, the lines here are blurry. We're not trying to make a claim that a new medication is going to reduce disease symptoms by X%. We're just trying to determine if there is a reasonable chance that X is causing Y, so that we can put the right solutions in place. The costs of being wrong here are much lower than in the scientific research community. This is why we aren't going to design experiments to test our hypothesis (although this is a legitimate option for Blackbelts!), instead we are going to use the information available to find the best evidence that we can to move forward (or not move forward) with a potential root cause.

Below is a chart with the tools that we will discuss for verifying potential root causes. The chart indicates that the tools on the left have less statistical rigor and therefore less certainty of a relationship than those to the right. You might want to choose a tool from the right if there are large financial implications associated with your project and therefore you want to be confident that the root causes you've identified are accurate. Follow the chart (the how-to) for each of the tools listed (minus workload analysis – which we talked about in the Lean section). Read more about each tool to understand when they would be most helpful in your project.

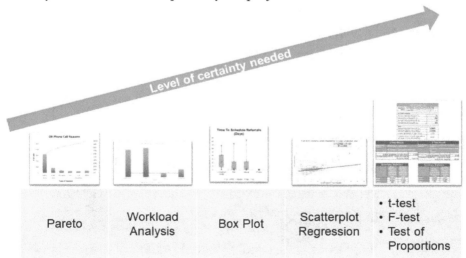

Tool: Pareto Chart

PURPOSE: The Pareto chart is a graphical tool meant to determine if the Pareto principle holds for the given problem. The Pareto principle states that 20% of the sources are responsible for 80% of the problem. This chart will determine if the principle is true for the data being analyzed, pointing to the "vital few" contributors to focus on eliminating. The Pareto chart is used for discrete data (typically count data separated into a handful of categories).

HOW TO COMPLETE:

1. Using Microsoft Excel, with the SPC XL add-in enabled, have one column of data that contains all of the categorical count information.

2. Click on the "SigmaZone" tab at the top, select the "Analysis Diagrams" dropdown menu, then choose "Pareto Chart".

3. Select the data range – this should include all of the categorical responses but should NOT include the title or header associated with the data. Excel will automatically count the number of times that each response is listed (do not try to do the Pareto with summarized data as it can sometimes create an error). Click "Next".

4. A box will pop up asking about chart settings. Once selections have been made, click "Next".

    a. **Sort Order:** Descending is the typical way that a Pareto is created. This shows the highest contributing categories first. Alternatively, this can be looked at in ascending order, where the highest contributing categories will appear last.

b. **Bar Type:** The default setting (and recommended setting for a Pareto Chart) is the "2-D Bars w Cum Line". The cumulative line is charted on a third axis that shows the percentage explained by the categories as you add them together from left to right. This is useful in determining where 80% of the variation or problems are coming from. The other two options will not include this line and will either show 2-D or 3-D bars depending on the selection.

c. **Gap Width:** Adjusting the gap width down will make the bars wider and the space between them narrower. Adjusting the gap width up will make the bars narrower and the space between them wider.

d. **# of Groups:** If there were responses that only showed up once or twice, Excel might automatically group them into an "other" category. By increasing the number of groups, Excel will split some of those back out individually, and by decreasing the number of groups, Excel will collapse more responses into the "other" category.

e. There is also an option to save default settings and ask not to see this pop-up box again.

5. The third box allows an opportunity to name the chart as well as the X-axis and the Y-axis.

a. There is also an option that is checked called "Create Pareto Report". This report will open in another worksheet and will summarize the percentage associated with each category in an Excel table. This can be unchecked if it is not desired. Click "Finish".

Tips:

- The chart and axes can be labeled after the creation of the chart. If "Finish" is clicked after the second box or if titles are not chosen until after the chart has been created, simply edit by double-clicking on the text.

- If you right-click on a bar in the chart, you can add data labels to enhance readability of the visual display.

- If one category is much larger than the others, it might be necessary to dig deeper into that category to understand more specifically what is going on that might be contributing to the problem. For example, if the OR is responsible for 70% of infections, perhaps that can be broken up to look at contributions by specialty service.

- If there does not appear to be a clear difference between the categories, it might be useful to stratify the data in another way. In the previous example, perhaps looking at the data by department does not show any differences, but breaking it up by individual surgeon might show clear contributors.

- Sometimes the highest contributing bar may not necessarily be the one that is most closely related to project goals. Keep this in mind and make sure that the team is still going after the right contributors to address the problem at hand.

- Assess whether or not the Pareto principle holds true for your data set. Do 20% of the categories or causes contribute to 80% or more of the effect? If so, your team has just gained keen insight into where to focus your improvement effort and energy.

Example:
Pathway to Discharge

The project team did a chart review on 50 discharges that occurred after 11AM. 25 discharges from each unit were evaluated to determine why discharge occurred after 11AM. The group categorized the contributing causes to the late discharge and created a Pareto diagram of their findings.

The team's chart did not follow the Pareto principle but did present some interesting findings. During the chart review, the team found that many patients were being delayed in discharge because they needed one last imaging study prior to being approved for discharge. Based on these findings, one of the team members met with Radiology to learn more about their workflow and prioritization process for studies. They discovered that radiology did not have visibility or knowledge of the fact that a patient was being planned for discharge.

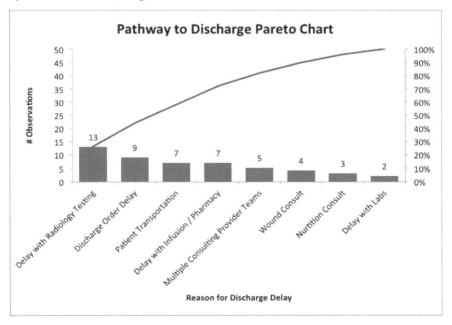

Tool: Box Plot

PURPOSE: A box plot is a graphical tool that is used to help visually show the difference between data sets. A box plot will show the median of each data set as well as the spread. Often referred to as "a box and whiskers plot", the "box" will show the middle 50% of the data, while the "whiskers" will extend to show the full range of the data set. Being able to look at the distribution of multiple data sets side by side can help to highlight their differences. Box plots are helpful when you have continuous data or count data that you want to separate into categories.

HOW TO COMPLETE:

1. Using Microsoft Excel, with the SPC XL add-in enabled, set up the data in columns (each data set should be in a separate column, all next to each other). If the data is already in a workbook in columns, this can be done from the original workbook.

2. Click on the "SigmaZone" tab at the top, select the "Analysis Diagrams" dropdown menu, then choose "Box Plot".

3. A box will pop up asking for the data range. Select all columns of data, including the headers. Then click "Next". Another box will appear asking about the orientation of the data. Because the data was already set up in columns, choose "Data sets in columns" and click "Next".

4. The box plot will open in a new worksheet.

Tips:

- The box represents the middle 50% of the data and the symbol in the box represents the median. The lines on either side represent the bottom and top 25% of the data. The box is a great visual for the interquartile range.

- While this diagram is useful to compare multiple data sets, keep in mind that clear differences in the shape of the plots do not necessarily mean that the groups are statistically significantly different from each other. A statistical hypothesis test should be run before claiming any true differences in the data (see T-test or F-test instructions).

- When looking at a box plot, you should be able to get a general sense if the spread or center of the data is different for each of the categories. This can help support a hypothesis that one category of data is different from the others.

Example:
Ophthalmology Clinic Flow

The Ophthalmology project team used a box plot to look at ap-pointment volumes by day of the week. The hypothesis was that appointment volumes would be highest on Wednesdays (thus patients would wait longer) and that they would be lowest on Fridays (thus patients would not have long waits on a Friday). The box plot does not support this hypothesis. The median number of appointments appears to be relatively stable across all days, with the lowest being on Monday. Variation on Thursday and Friday is slightly larger than the other days, with Friday having some days with less appointments than other days. This resulted in the team focusing on clinic flow as a whole rather than being tempted to address individual days.

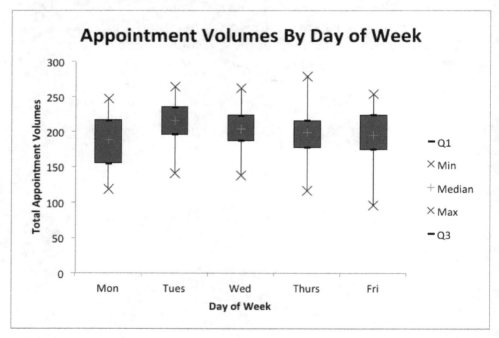

Tool: Scatterplot and Regression

PURPOSE: A scatterplot is a graphical tool used to look for a possible relationship between two continuous variables. The scatterplot can be used to confirm a hypothesis that two variables might be related. A scatterplot DOES NOT necessarily indicate a causal relationship. X could be causing Y, but Y could also be causing X, or a third variable may be responsible for the changes in both X and Y. A scatterplot (and the associated regression analysis) should be used to determine if there is a relationship between your potential root cause and the problem, but should not assume causality.

HOW TO COMPLETE:

1. Using Microsoft Excel, with the SPC XL add-in enabled, set up the data in two columns representing the two continuous variables. If the data is already in a workbook in two columns, this can be done from the original workbook.

2. Click on the "SigmaZone" tab at the top, select the "Analysis Diagrams" dropdown menu, then choose "Scatterplot".

3. A box will pop up asking for the data range. Select all of the data in both columns, including the headers. Click "Next". The scatterplot will open in a new worksheet.

4. When the scatterplot is created it will plot a regression line and give the equation of that line. It will also automatically list R-squared on the chart. This value represents the amount of the variation in Y that can be explained by the linear relationship with X. This number ranges from 0 to 1.

a. The closer R-squared is to the number 1, the stronger the relationship between the two variables. The direction of the line indicates whether the relationship is positive or negative. A line slanted upwards indicates a positive relationship – an increase in one variable is related to an increase in the other variable. A line slanted downwards indicates a negative relationship – an increase in one variable is related to a decrease in the other variable.

Tips:

- When looking at the scatterplot, the closer the dots are clustered together, the stronger the correlation. A scatterplot that has dots all over the graph with no rhyme nor reason, likely represents two variables that are not related to one another. (Review the following visuals as an example.)

- Remember that a strong correlation still does not necessarily represent a causal relationship. However, the stronger the correlation, the more confidence that the two variables are related to each other.

- If there is no correlation, consider other ways to break up the data to test for a possible relationship. If the data can be broken into categories, consider multiple scatterplots side-by-side or a box plot to verify a relationship.

- A regression analysis can also be completed in SPC XL without the creation of a scatterplot.

To do this the data still needs to be formatted in two columns but the directions would be:

- Click on the "SigmaZone" tab at the top, select the "Analysis Tools" dropdown menu, then choose "Multiple Regression".

- A box will pop up asking for the data range. Select all of the data in both columns, including the headers. Click "Next". The regression output will open in a new worksheet.

R-SQUARED	STRENGTH OF CORRELATION
1.0	Perfect correlation
.8	Strong correlation
.6	Moderately strong
.4	Moderate correlation
.2	Weak correlation
0	No correlation

COMMON SCATTERPLOT PATTERNS

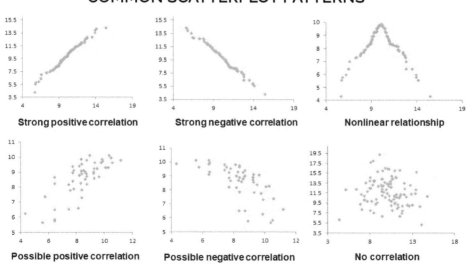

Strong positive correlation   Strong negative correlation   Nonlinear relationship

Possible positive correlation   Possible negative correlation   No correlation

Example:
Pathway to Discharge

One question among the Pathway to Discharge team was if patients with a longer length of stay would be discharged closer to the expected 11AM time. This was due to the fact that patients staying in the hospital for multiple days had more time to plan for discharge with their care teams, whereas patients with relatively short stays might not complete discharge planning with the care team. The results of the scatterplot below show an R-squared of .0134. This indicates that there is no relationship between the two variables shown (length of stay in days and time past expected discharge in hours).

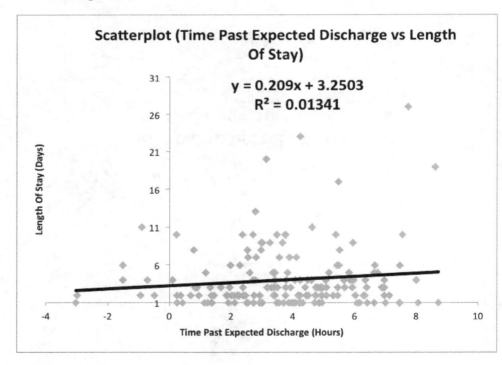

Now you have half of the tools in your root cause verification toolkit. The last three tools all fall under the umbrella of formal hypothesis testing. These tools are often used in research and provide an additional level of certainty to a relationship that the other tools we have discussed are not able to provide. They indicate whether groups of data are different enough from each other to claim that the difference is statistically significant. I know, it seemed like we were done with all of the mathematical explanations, but we've got one more for you. This is it and then it is all smooth sailing from here!

But why should you listen to us? Why should you even care about statistical significance? Well, you could just take our word for it since we haven't steered you wrong yet! Or, you can read our brief (and really awesome!) answer: Statistical significance means that the groups are truly different from each other and not just appearing to be different due to random chance or sampling bias. Without statistical significance we could overreact or underreact to a potential relationship. Both overreacting and underreacting could have serious implications depending on the situation. Look at these examples below.

EXAMPLE ONE:

There might appear to be a difference between patient satisfaction scores for clinics that have an automated-call distribution (ACD) phone system and those that do not. If it appears that the ACD phone systems are related to higher patient satisfaction scores, we might invest time, money, and resources into implementing this throughout an organization. However, what if that difference is only marginal? What if we are drawing conclusions about a difference that isn't great enough to warrant the cost of the change?

SCENARIO	REACTION	MATHEMATICAL PHRASING
Acting when there is no true difference	Overreacting	Type I error

EXAMPLE TWO:

Perhaps a box plot shows that there is a slight difference in mortality rates for patients who receive the Sepsis bundle and patients who do not receive the Sepsis bundle. Because bundle implementation is resource intensive and difficult to maintain, an organization might decide that the difference is not great enough to warrant this expense. However, what if the difference is greater than it appears to be? Perhaps there is a statistically significant difference and implementing the bundle effectively could reduce mortality rates.

SCENARIO	REACTION	MATHEMATICAL PHRASING
Failing to act when there is a difference	Underreacting	Type II error

When it comes to testing a hypothesis, these are some terms to know:

- **Null hypothesis (H_0):** there is no significant difference between the groups
- **Alternative Hypothesis (Ha):** there is a significant difference between the groups
- The output of a statistical hypothesis test indicates a **p-value.** The p-value represents the strength of the evidence against the null hypothesis (meaning that the groups are different)
- **p-value >.05** – retain the null hypothesis (the groups are not different) – "if the p is high, let the null fly"
- **p-value <.05** – reject the null hypothesis (the groups are different) – "if the p is low, the null must go"

When testing a hypothesis, we decide what an acceptable error rate is for a test (**alpha**). For the purposes of process improvement work, an error rate of 5% is generally deemed acceptable. This is why a p-value of less than .05 indicates a statistically significant difference. A helpful way to think about hypothesis testing is to liken it to the structure of the U.S. Criminal Justice System. In criminal court, the burden falls on the prosecution to show, beyond reasonable doubt (the "alpha" in a court case), that the defendant is guilty. In a hypothesis test, the goal is to show, beyond reasonable doubt (.05), that the groups are different. Look at the examples below to review similarities between the two situations and the possible outcomes (Privitera, 2018)[2].

Courtroom:

Alternative hypothesis: The defendant is guilty
Null hypothesis: The defendant is innocent (What we assume going into the trial)

		TRUTH	
		Innocent	**Guilty**
Jury Decision	**Innocent**	Freed an innocent person Correct	Freed a guilty person Type II error
	Guilty	Convicted an innocent person Type I error	Convicted a guilty person Correct

The question to answer is whether or not there is enough evidence against the defendant to reject the null hypothesis that he/she is innocent? Now look at the same information for a hypothesis test.

Hypothesis test:

Alternative hypothesis: There is a difference between groups
Null hypothesis: There is no difference between groups (What we should assume going into a hypothesis test)

		TRUTH	
		H_0: no difference	**H_a: difference**
Test Result	**P>.05 (retain)**	Retained the null, the groups are not different Correct	Retained the null, but there is a true difference Type II error
	P<.05 (reject)	Rejected the null, when there is not a true difference Type I error	Rejected the null, the groups are different Correct

2 Privitera, G.J. (2018). *Statistics for the Behavior Sciences, 3rd Ed.* Sage Publications, United States.

The question to answer is whether or not there is enough evidence to indicate that the two groups are truly different. If we are wrong, we might make changes that are not really going to have an impact (type I error) or fail to make changes that could have helped (type II error).

The three hypothesis tests that we are going to cover are used when you have two groups of data and you want to determine if the two groups are different. If you have more than two groups of data, a more advanced statistical test is necessary (often an Analysis of Variance or ANOVA). We are not going to cover those in this book, there are many books on statistics that can help you better understand how to perform those tests – or ask a Blackbelt! Use the chart below as a reference for which test to use when comparing two groups of data.

Hypothesis Test	Comparing
t-test	Means
F-test	Variances
Test of Proportions	Percentages

Tool: t-test or F-test

PURPOSE: Both the t-test and the F-test are statistical tests than can be run to determine if there is a statistically significant difference between two sets of continuous data. While a t-test looks at the means, the F-test looks at the standard deviation or variance within the groups. If a hypothesis test is run and the p-value is less than .05, this means that there is a 95% chance that the groups are truly different and are not different due to random chance. This is important because while two groups can appear to be different, a statistical test can help support that they truly are different with 95% confidence.

HOW TO COMPLETE:

1. Using Microsoft Excel, with the SPC XL add-in enabled, set up the data in two columns representing the two data sets to compare. If the data is already in a workbook in two columns, this can be done from the original workbook.

2. Click on the "SigmaZone" tab at the top, select the "Analysis Tools" dropdown menu, then choose "t-test matrix" or "F-test matrix" depending on the intended test.

3. A box will pop up asking for the data range. Select both columns of data in full, including headers. A second box will appear asking about the orientation of columns. Because the data is already set up in columns, choose "Data in Columns".

4. A third box will appear asking which alternative hypothesis should be tested.

    a. For every hypothesis test there is a null hypothesis H_0 and an alternative hypothesis Ha. The alternative hypothesis is the predicted difference between the means (or standard deviations). The null hypothesis always states that there is no difference between the two groups.

    b. SPC XL is asking if one group is predicted to be higher than the other, or if the prediction is simply that the groups are not equal. Depending on the expected differences between the two groups, select which alternative hypothesis is appropriate for the test. Click "OK".

5. A test result will open in a new worksheet. This result will give you the p-value and the confidence value. In order to claim that the difference between the two groups is statistically significant, the p-value would need to be less than .05. The test results will also give a summary box which will show the mean, standard deviation, and total count of values for each of the two groups. See the example for an output of both an F-test and a t-test.

$$Tips:$$

- A t-test compares the means of two groups, while the F-test compares the variance (or standard deviation).

- Note: The t-test and F-test can only be used when looking at the difference between two groups of data. When comparing more than two groups, an Analysis of Variance (ANOVA) test or other advanced statistical test should be run.

- If the p-value is <.05 the null hypothesis is rejected – this means that the test provides support for the alternate hypothesis. Note that this doesn't "prove" a difference, but strongly supports one.

- If the p-value is >.05 the null hypothesis must be retained – this means that the test does not provide support for the alternative hypothesis. While the groups may appear different from one another, that could be due to random chance rather than a true statistically significant difference.

- Both the F-test and the t-test are used for continuous data; when working with discrete data a test of proportions should be used.

Example:
Ophthalmology Clinic Flow

Remember the box plot we made earlier looking at the difference in appointment volumes by day of the week? That box plot appeared to show that there was no difference between the number of appointments scheduled on each day. However, some members of the team were still convinced that Fridays just weren't as busy as the other days. It is important to listen to team members when they feel that the data doesn't match what they are seeing and feeling. So instead of looking at volumes, we decided to look at the difference in patient wait times on a Friday (the day that staff felt they were least busy) and compared that to patient wait times on a Wednesday (the day that staff felt they were most busy in clinic). Below are the t-test (comparing means) and F-test (comparing variation) results.

t-Test Result		
Hypothesis Tested:	H0: Wednesday Mean = Friday Mean	
	H1: Wednesday Mean not equal to Friday Mean	
p-value (probability of Type I Error)		0.591
Confidence that Wednesday Mean not equal to Friday Mean		40.9%

Summary Statistics		
	Wednesday	Friday
Mean	117.053	115.167
StDev	21.954	20.473
Count	75	72

The results above represent the p-values from a two sample, 2-tailed t-test. This means that the probability of falsely concluding the alternative hypothesis is the value shown (where the alternate hypothesis is that the means are not equal).

		True State of Nature	
		H0	H1
Conclusion	H0	Correct	Type II Error
Drawn	H1	Type I Error	Correct

F-Test Result

| Hypothesis Tested: | H0: Wednesday Variance = Friday Variance |
| | H1: Wednesday Variance not equal to Friday Variance |

p-value (probability of Type I Error)	0.555
Confidence that Wednesday Variance not equal to Friday Variance	44.5%

Summary Statistics

	Wednesday	Friday
Mean	117.053	115.167
StDev	21.954	20.473
Count	75	72

The results above represent the p-values from a two sample, 2-tailed F-test. This means that the probability of falsely concluding the alternative hypothesis is the value shown (where the alternate hypothesis is that the variances are not equal).

		True State of Nature	
		HO	H1
Conclusion	HO	Correct	Type II Error
Drawn	H1	Type I Error	Correct

The p-value for both tests was greater than .05, showing that Wednesdays and Fridays truly did not differ in terms of patient wait times. This was important for members of the team to see. This helped them to understand that there must be another reason why Fridays did not feel as busy as Wednesdays because there was no difference in volumes (as seen in the box plot) and no difference in patient wait times (as seen in the t and F tests).

Tool: Test of Proportions

PURPOSE: The test of proportions is a statistical test that is run to determine if there is a statistically significant difference between two sets of data, when the data is discrete. This hypothesis test compares the difference in proportion between the two groups. If a hypothesis test is run and the p-value is less than .05, this means that there is a 95% chance that the groups are truly different and are not different due to random chance. This is important because while two groups can appear to be different, a statistical test can help support that they truly are different with 95% confidence.

HOW TO COMPLETE:

1. Using Microsoft Excel, with the SPC XL add-in enabled, complete some basic count exercises. Count the total number of samples in each group (=COUNT) and then count the number of samples that have the given characteristic being studied.

2. Click on the "SigmaZone" tab at the top, select the "Analysis Tools" dropdown menu, then choose "Test of Proportions".

3. A box will pop up asking which alternate hypothesis should be tested.

   a. For every hypothesis test there is a null hypothesis H_0 and an alternate hypothesis Ha. The alternate hypothesis is the predicted difference between the proportions. The null hypothesis always states that there is no difference between the two groups.

b. SPC XL is asking if one proportion is predicted to be higher than the other, or if the prediction is simply that the proportions are not equal. Depending on the expected differences between the two groups, select which alternate hypothesis is appropriate for the test. Click "OK".

4. A new worksheet will open with a Test of Proportions calculator. This will look similar to final reports for other test outputs, but is actually the calculator where the count data should be entered (see example).

5. Use the yellow-highlighted boxes to input count data. The "Sample Size" for each group is the total count of all samples in that group. The "Number Defective" is the number of instances of a given characteristic for each group.

a. Please note that "Defective" could be a misnomer. Perhaps the test is looking at whether or not there is a difference between the number of providers in two different groups. The "Number Defective" would be the number of instances of a provider in each group, which is not to say that the provider is a defect, but is simply the target variable in the test.

6. As numbers are entered into the yellow fields, the results box will populate below. A p-value of less than .05 indicates that there is a statistically significant difference between the two groups.

Tips:

- The test of proportions is used for determining the difference between two groups whose data is discrete. An example of this might be that 50% of a given population has x disease. Perhaps there is a desire to know if that group is statistically different from another population where only 30% of the population has the disease. This would allow for some comparisons to be made regarding why the proportion of diseased individuals is higher than the other.

- If the p-value is <.05, the null hypothesis is rejected – this means that the test provides support for the alternate hypothesis. Note that this doesn't "prove" a difference, but strongly supports one.

- If the p-value is >.05, the null hypothesis must be retained – this means that the test does not provide support for the alternate hypothesis. While the groups may appear different from one another, that could be due to random chance rather than a true statistically significant difference.

- The test of proportions is used for discrete data. If the variable being compared is continuous, either the F-test or the t-test should be used instead.

- If more than two groups need to be compared, an advanced test is needed.

Example:
Pathway to Discharge

The Pathway to Discharge team was interested in better understanding whether or not there was a statistically significant difference between the number of on-time discharges between the two surgical units. This interest stemmed from work to validate the potential root cause that the variation in provider rounding structure and timing had an impact on on-time discharges. To test the alternative hypothesis that the two units had a statistically significant difference in number of on-time discharges, they utilized a test of proportions. Results are shown below.

Key for interpretation:
Group 1 = Unit 1N
Group 2 = Unit 3N
Defective = discharge time after 11:00AM

The resulting p-value was found to be 0.361. This value is greater than 0.05, which means that we should not reject the null hypothesis in favor of the alternative, the evidence is not there to support that the two units have a different number of on-time discharges. The team went on to analyze this same data by surgical service (vascular surgery, general surgery, etc.) to see if they could find any additional insight into causal factors.

Test of Proportions

Hypothesis Tested: H0: Group #1 Proportion = Group #2 Proportion
H1: Group #1 Proportion not equal to Group #2 Proportion

User defined parameters	
Number Defective Group #1 (x_1)	178
Sample Size of Group #1 (n_1)	192
Number Defective Group #2 (x_2)	501
Sample Size of Group #2 (n_2)	530

Results	
Sample Proportion Group #1 (p_1)	0.92708
Sample Proportion Group #2 (p_2)	0.94528
p-value (probability of Type I Error)	0.361
Confidence that Group #1 proportion is not equal to Group #2 proportion	63.9%

		True State of Nature	
		H0	H1
Conclusion	H0	Correct	Type II Error
Drawn	H1	Type I Error	Correct

Once you have used some of these tools to verify root causes, you should have a list of the root causes to address in Improve. When you move to the Improve phase you want to be sure to aim improvements at these root causes that you verified, so don't try to sneak any others through!

Here are some questions to ask yourself when you think you're ready to move from Analyze to Improve:

- What are the potential root causes of the problem?
- What are the verified root causes of the problem?
- What are the critical few root causes to address in Improve?
- Are there opportunities to apply Lean principles to the process?

Once you can answer those, you are ready to move to Improve, which means taking action against your problem!

Chapter Five:
Improve

You have finally reached the Improve phase! The phase you've been waiting for all along, right? Hint: if you skipped right to this chapter because you think the prework is a waste of time – you're doing it wrong. Everything that you've done up until this point is value added in solving the problem you have identified. Now it's time to compile all of that information and help find the right solution (or two, or three). You can think about breaking up your Improve work into four key areas of focus: developing potential solutions, evaluating potential solutions, testing solutions, and implementing. By the time you finish the Improve phase you'll have found a solution that works for your problem! (I know this because you literally cannot move to the next phase until you have found some form of success, therefore this phase is practically stamped with "success guaranteed".)

DEVELOPING POTENTIAL SOLUTIONS

Do you remember all that math you did in Analyze to verify your root causes? (Honestly, how could you forget it? It's intense!) Well, it's time to put that to good use! Now you know what some of the key reasons for your problem are and you can work to specifically eliminate those causes. We know at least one person is going to read this chapter and be thinking "I didn't do the math...what are they talking about?" We know who you are, we've had students like you before. If you feel like you found the right root causes even though you skipped the math, then I suppose you can keep reading (but not without a tsk, tsk). With the root causes of the problem identified, solutions can be generated to target those causes by integrating Lean solutions, benchmarking for existing solutions, or generating brand new solutions.

We talked about Lean a lot in Analyze. With its focus on removing waste and adding value, there are a lot of great ways to use Lean to analyze and understand a process. There are also a lot of Lean solutions that have been used in various settings over the years as a way to maximize the process. We will talk through some of the common Lean solutions that might be applicable in a healthcare project. The first is workload balancing.

Workload balancing is the improvement half of workload analysis, which we discussed in the last chapter. You complete a workload analysis to understand the problem and assess improvement opportunities. If you identified through a workload analysis that certain steps of the process were performing under or over takt time, then you might want to consider workload balancing as an option in Improve. There isn't really a separate tool for workload balancing, but rather you build off of the workload analysis tool that you already created. Review the work that occurs at each step and look for opportunities to adjust. Was there duplicate work that can be eliminated? Is someone who is performing under takt time qualified to complete a task that is currently assigned to someone who is performing over takt time? Play with combinations of rebalancing the work and then check for a new comparison to takt time. Additionally, if you believe that the work is as lean as it gets, but you are still not meeting takt time, you can use the workload analysis and any balancing attempts as part of your business case for requesting additional resources.

Balancing work by using the workload analysis as your foundation can be really beneficial for creating a smoother process. It will help eliminate bottlenecks, rework, and overburden while also giving you or the leader in that business unit an accurate assessment of how many resources are needed to complete the tasks assigned while meeting demand.

A tool that can be used to think about tactics for managing workload is called an ECRS. Check out the tool callout box to learn more.

Tool: ECRS

PURPOSE: To identify where waste occurs in a process and determine options for eliminating, combining, rearranging, or simplifying steps in order to reduce waste.

HOW TO COMPLETE:

1. First, identify the work elements to be considered for elimination, combination, rearrangement, or simplification. List these in the first blank column.

2. Indicate the type of waste that is present in the task as it is currently being done.

3. Indicate the idea for improving this task and removing the waste.

4. Then choose which of the four techniques is being utilized for this task:

    a. Eliminate – identify steps that can be quickly eliminated

    b. Combine – seek to combine steps and think about who, what, and when

    c. Rearrange – consider rearranging the order of work

    d. Simplify – try to reduce complexity of the work

Tips:

- This is a tool that is typically used to help organize team ideas around specific steps. Sometimes, multiple improvement ideas might be present for a step. There might be one idea for eliminating it and another for combining it with a different step. List these individually so that teams can see all of the options available.

Example:
Ophthalmology Clinic Flow

The Ophthalmology project team used an ECRS to think about elements of the technician workup and create a standard workup for patients that was streamlined.

Work Analysis				Eliminate	Combine	Rearrange	Simplify
#	Work Elements	Waste or Inefficiency	Improvement Idea	E	C	R	S
1	Dilation of patients having eyes examined	Waiting - patients wait 20 minutes for eyes to dialate	Perform this at the beginning of the technician workup instead of the end			X	
2	Medical history review	Overprocessing - entering this into two locations in the EMR	Decide which location is used by the provider and educate staff on where to perform this task	X			X
3	Medication review	Non-utilized talent, overprocessing - currently done by providers and technicians	Technicians complete medication review during workup and consult providers if necessary	X	X		

Another Lean tool that should be considered during the Improve phase is mistake proofing. This is particularly useful if you're trying to remove defects from a process. Mistake proofing is pretty self-explanatory and I'm confident that you have encountered this in one way, shape, or form at some point in your life. You may have even referred to mistake proofing techniques as idiot proofing somewhere along the way. We, of course, have never done that, because we are objectively nice people. But call it what you will – the idea is to stop a mistake from happening. You can utilize technology, process checks, or other methods to either prevent, detect, or minimize the effects of mistakes.

Most of the time when people make mistakes it isn't because of negligence or carelessness, but because of performing tasks on auto-pilot. Introducing something that causes them to stop and think, can often help reduce the risk of a mistake. When considering mistake proofing as a solution, always think about the cost/benefit analysis. If the consequences of a mistake are minor, it might not be worth a large or expensive effort to implement a mistake proofing technique. For example, if you had a railroad crossing in a large metropolitan area, you would likely spend the money to have rails installed, flashing lights, perhaps even a noise indicator (such as bells or alarms). In a rural area all of that might not be necessary, you might simply have a noise indicator and a sign. There are three levels of mistake proofing; review the chart to see the distinctions and some healthcare examples.

LEVEL OF MISTAKE PROOFING	DEFINITION	EXAMPLE
Level 3 – "Good"	Detects a mistake that has resulted in a defect and prevents the defect from causing harm	**Barcode Medication Administration:** The defect has already occurred in pulling the incorrect medication from the storage area, but if the barcode doesn't match, this stops the nurse from continuing with the mistake and causing harm by administering the medication to the patient.
Level 2 – "Better"	Detects a mistake before it results in a defect	**Lab alarm:** For certain lab specimens that need to be processed quickly to maintain integrity, our Pathology department has a light that flashes when the specimen arrives to alert staff. If the specimen sits for too long (but before it would be unusable), an alarm will sound to notify staff of the mistake and alert them that the specimen needs to be processed immediately. The mistake was made – the specimen wasn't processed in the preferred timeframe, but the defect of an unusable specimen has not occurred.
Level 1 – "Best"	Prevents a mistake from ever occurring	**Oxygen and CO2 Connectors:** The holes to connect these are different shapes and sizes so that you cannot connect CO2 when trying to connect Oxygen.

A Lean concept called jidoka is also something that could be incorporated into potential solutions during the Improve phase. Jidoka is the ability to detect errors and immediately stop the work, similar to a "stop the line" concept in manufacturing. If you're making cars and you notice that a machine is not functioning properly, you want to stop the line and fix the machine to prevent each car on the line from being affected. The same should be true for our processes in healthcare. If we see a safety concern or something that is causing errors, we should all (regardless of our role!) feel comfortable speaking up and identifying the concern. This can help to decrease harm and/or future rework. Utilizing a concept called humble inquiry – asking questions to learn and understand – can be a helpful way of doing this. Utilizing jidoka in healthcare does require a culture that supports it, but all healthcare organizations should be striving towards that culture.

One last Lean tool to consider in the Improve phase is 5S. 5S is also a fantastic standalone tool. Seriously, you can (and probably should) utilize this tool over and over again as a standalone effort. We've done several standalone 5S projects and we have also done 5S work as part of the Improve phase of larger projects. We have also used 5S on things like our holiday wrapping materials, our kitchens, our digital workspaces – oh, boy, the list is endless! 5S can be seriously addicting if you like organizing or having an organized space. In healthcare, 5S can be helpful in removing clutter and keeping your area in compliance with regulations from various accrediting bodies.

5S is a simple, yet highly effective technique that will help you to remove waste from your environment by creating better workplace organization and visual management. If you identified root causes related to people needing to search to find stuff, too much clutter, not having exam rooms set up with the correct materials, or other causes surrounding "stuff", then 5S might be a solution to consider. Review the next table to see the five steps of 5S work.

5S STEP	OVERVIEW	DETAILS
Sort	Remove all items that are not needed for current work. Eliminate clutter and free up space.	Identify, tag, and remove unneeded items from the workspace – hold them for a period of time (2-4 weeks) to see if they are needed. Remove old or obsolete equipment. Determine necessary quantities. Ask yourself how often items are needed, how many of each are really needed, are there broken or obsolete items that can be removed?
Set In Order	Arrange materials and supplies efficiently and safely, creating a place for everything close to where it is used.	Think about the flow of the space, arrange items in a way that makes them easy to locate. Heavily accessed items should be between shoulder and waist level for minimum motion. Use labeling and taping to clearly mark "homes" for items.
Shine	Regularly clean and maintain the workplace and equipment to keep it in a 'like new' condition.	Keep the place clean and safe. Regularly clean the space for dirt and grime. Inspect tools and equipment to ensure that they are working. Keep wires bundled and in a safe location.
Standardize	Set expectations and standards to ensure that this new level of organization, cleanliness, and waste elimination is maintained.	Create standards or rules for the space to ensure that everyone maintains the new, organized environment. Use visual management. Consider a "drop box" space for people to return items when they are unsure of their proper location. Adjust your standard as staff interact with the space and identify necessary tweaks.
Sustain	Conduct audits to evaluate, give feedback, and communicate performance. This requires discipline!	Regularly audit the space (see tool below) to ensure that the efforts are maintained. Ensure that staff and leadership have clearly identified roles in maintaining the 5S work.

5S can help improve safety, establish convenient and standard processes, increase product quality (helping you identify expired products!), and empower staff to maintain their own work area. The beauty of it is really that it can be done almost anywhere. You can do this in supply rooms, exam rooms, nursing stations, break rooms, procedure carts – really, anywhere! You can 5S things big or small or even your digital space (seriously, we applied these concepts to our SharePoint site and it worked great!).

In our organization we use this audit tool to determine what spaces might need 5S and then to perform regular audits of the space to assess sustainability. The tool can be modified with questions that are appropriate for your area.

5S Audit Metrics

Area:		Ratings		Date			
		Very Poor - 1, Poor - 2, Good - 3, Very Good - 4, Excellent - 5					
Sort	Are needed items present in the right quantities?						
	Are unneeded items (supplies, equipment, furniture, etc.) present?						
	Are display boards up to date?						
	Are items present where they shouldn't be (in aisles, hallways, corners, on counters, etc.)?						
	Are safety hazards (cords, leads, blocked: egress, extinguishers, pull stations, etc.) present?						
Set in Order	Are items in convenient locations for easy access?						
	Are items put away after use?						
	Are walkways and/or equipment identified?						
	Are there overstuffed drawers, shelves, and/or supply closets?						
	Are missing or misplaced items easy to identify?						
Shine	Are floors, walls, stairs, counters, tables, other surfaces dirty or messy?						
	Is equipment dusty or dirty?						
	Is equipment in need of repair? Have workorders been placed?						
	Are facilities in need of repair? Does the building look in like new condition?						
Standardize	Is work information visible at a glance?						
	Are 5S standards known, posted or visible at a glance?						
	Are job aids (checklists, flowcharts, diagrams, instructions, etc.) visible?						
	Is 5S audit data and information posted and current?						
	Are there items that cannot be located within seconds?						
Sustain	Can employees explain the value of 5S?						
	Is 5S performed routinely or daily?						
	Are success stories displayed? Is 5S part of regular departmental communication?						
	Have there been improvements to the 5S system?						
	Is everyone's role clearly defined?						
	Audit Score:	0	0	0	0	0	
90-115: On Target Good Work!	65-89: Getting There, Continue to Reinforce 5S Standards			<65: Beginning or Higher Effort Required			

Throughout this book we have been walking you through two projects. The Ophthalmology project did end up benefiting from some 5S work for the imaging spaces. We saw a great improvement in reducing outdated equipment and clutter and making it easier for staff to do their work in the space provided. While the team did a great job performing 5S work as one of the improvements, we seriously failed at taking pictures. We literally took none. Sadly, this happens a lot. You start doing the work and totally forget how awesome a before and after photo would be. So instead of sharing photos from the Ophthalmology work, we are showing you photos from our very own supply area. In the Value Institute Learning Center we have supplies, a lot of supplies, that we use for classes and for our own project work. As much as we love doing 5S for other teams, it was high-time we did it to our own stuff. We finally did and here is the result.

BEFORE

AFTER

We are all so much happier with the new space and it makes getting materials ready for class so much easier!

While there are several Lean solutions that can be integrated into your improvement efforts, there are also a lot of fantastic processes that are already functioning well. Talking to others about solutions that have already been successful at solving similar problems is called benchmarking. Benchmarking is extremely useful and prevents you from reinventing the wheel when techniques from others could be utilized to help address the problem that you are trying to solve. You can benchmark internally with other departments in your organization, or externally with other organizations. This is an effort that can be done not only by the team leader, but also by team members.

Internal benchmarking can be very deliberate or can happen by chance. For example, a team member on a Medical Infusion project might know someone who works in the Oncology department. He/she might have an idea about something in Oncology infusion that could be applied to Medical Infusion to help address the problem. This is an opportunity that should be seized! Encourage team members who are aware of other beneficial efforts, to connect with the appropriate people and find out more. A more deliberate approach might be looking at the performance of other departments to see if there are departments who are very successful at something you are struggling with. For example, if you are working on reducing central line infections on your inpatient unit, you might look at data for all of the inpatient units. Who has the lowest rates of central line infections? What are they doing differently? Sometimes this is referred to as positive deviance. If someone is doing something well, recognize them and learn from them! It's a win-win for both groups. Some organizations might even choose to be really proactive and schedule regular sharing sessions among similar departments.

The ways in which you can approach external benchmarking are very similar. You can proactively look for solutions that might already exist by reading journal articles or case studies, attending conferences on a regular basis to hear about best practices, or connecting with organizations just to find out how they are addressing a common healthcare concern (such as access to outpatient clinic appointments). You can also happen upon opportunities for external benchmarking if you have team members that are aware of technology or techniques for addressing your current problem, they can reach out and get more information. We have had several people on our team over the years who have come from industries other than healthcare and they are always amazed at how open the healthcare community is in sharing best practices. People that work in healthcare are very people focused, and we all have similar goals – we want to do what is right for our patients. It is true that benchmarking in other industries can be difficult as people want to keep their trade secrets to themselves. We can honestly say that we have not run into that concern with benchmarking in our healthcare work. Most organizations will be happy to discuss their techniques and suggested best practices with you.

While benchmarking can be extremely beneficial, and we've seen a handful of projects that have benefited really well from a solution that was picked up via benchmarking, you also have to approach implementation of a benchmarked idea with some caution. You have done a lot of work up until this point to understand your problem and the current state of the process that you are working in. You don't want all of that to go to waste because you found a solution via benchmarking that you are just going to install in your area. Think about what you've learned and the root causes that you've identified. Can the solution be implemented as is or do you need to consider modifications? Oftentimes these solutions need to be adapted to fit our processes, constraints, or culture. Following the advice in the rest of this chapter is really important in successfully implementing any potential solutions, even benchmarked best practices.

A third technique for developing potential solutions is to brainstorm new ideas. Almost everyone that we've encountered has participated in some form of brainstorming before. It is used frequently for all sorts of things. You brainstorm places to go on vacation with your family. You brainstorm holiday gift ideas for friends. You probably already brainstorm solutions to problems at work too! What we want to provide you with is an explanation of some different methods for brainstorming that can be useful when working with your team. You should choose the technique based on the dynamics of the team that you have observed thus far. The most important rule of brainstorming is making sure that everyone gets to share their ideas, and that there is no criticism of those ideas at this stage. Benchmarked ideas and Lean solutions should be integrated into your final list of possible solutions, along with the ideas generated during the brainstorming session.

Tool: Brainstorming

PURPOSE: To generate a list of potential ideas or solutions for the problem.

HOW TO COMPLETE:

1. Choose a style of brainstorming that best fits the team: Round robin, popcorn, brainwriting, or silent idea generation.

2. Allow for silent thinking time (5-7 minutes) before starting the activity.

3. **Round Robin**

   a. Go around the table and take ideas from each person in order. People can pass if they do not have an idea. Write each idea on a poster or whiteboard. Continue going around the table until everyone has finished listing all of their ideas.

      i. Benefits: everyone has a turn to share

      ii. Drawbacks: everyone may not be comfortable sharing their ideas aloud, they might reserve ideas that they are embarrassed to share.

4. **Popcorn**

   a. Have everyone start calling out ideas with very little structure. Capture each idea on a poster or whiteboard. Continue until no one has ideas left to share.

      i. Benefits: people don't have to hold an idea until it is their turn, they can keep shouting them out as they think of new ideas.

    ii. Drawbacks: quieter team members might struggle with this. It might be difficult to get ideas out with other members constantly speaking up or people might not be comfortable sharing their ideas out loud.

5. **Brainwriting**

   a. Give every team member a piece of paper. Have them write down as many ideas as they can for one minute. Pass the paper to the left. Have everyone silently read the ideas on the paper in front of them and then generate new ideas for another minute. Keep going until everyone is out of ideas.

    i. Benefits: might make people more comfortable sharing ideas, allows people to build off the ideas of others.

    ii. Drawbacks: might not have the same level of energy as a verbal brainstorming session.

6. **Silent Idea Generation**

   a. Give each team member a stack of Post-It notes and have them silently generate as many ideas are they can (one per sticky). Let them brainstorm until everyone is finished generating ideas and then go through ideas aloud and place them on a board.

    i. Benefits: allows for quieter individuals to get out all of their ideas.

    ii. Drawbacks: some people still might not like being associated with their idea when it goes on the board, requires a bit more affinitizing by the facilitator as ideas are placed on the board.

Tips:

- Preface the activity with some ground rules specific to brainstorming: no idea is a bad or stupid idea, absolutely no judgement or critiquing of ideas at this stage, quantity is better than quality – ideas do not need to be detailed or fully fleshed-out.

- Record all ideas and try not to paraphrase – this can be a passive way of critiquing – write the idea down as it is worded by the team member.

- Do not allow for discussion of ideas at this time, focus only on generating new ideas.

Example:
Ophthalmology Clinic Flow

The Ophthalmology team brainstormed ideas for improvement using silent idea generation. They then organized their ideas into an affinity diagram. Note: OCT in the diagram below stands for "Optical Coherence Tomography" which is a type of imaging done in Ophthalmology.

Standardization	Technology	Tech Workflow
Standard one place to document referral information and previous medical records	Streamline HPI (history of present illness)/tech note and problem list	Feedback loop for techs
Offer to schedule patients when they are here	OCT in every work up room	Tech reporting structure update
Standard tech workup and room setup	Use TVs to update patients in a digital way	Clarify chief tech duties, delegate
Develop standard communication process	Go paperless – no more apt slips	**Environment**
Provider standard work	Create a survey better suited to eye clinic	Provide patients with entertainment during wait time
5S OCT rooms	Create a system to see that a patient has arrived	Visual management of patient flow
Standardize process of techs documenting in HPI (no more provider preference)	Change input order of HPI information on the EMR template (Move "Chief Complaint" sooner)	Clinic layout – flow design
Schedule OCT and workup		Combine all waiting rooms into one central suite

EVALUATING POTENTIAL SOLUTIONS

At this point you (hopefully) have many possible solutions on the table. There are generally a lot of possible solutions that could help to solve any given problem. But unless you are some kind of superhero (Fact: if you really had cool powers, you wouldn't be reading this book to solve a problem), you cannot possibly implement every idea that was generated. Some of the ideas might even conflict – where you would choose either this or that, but not both. This is why it is helpful to have a couple of tools available for evaluating potential solutions.

Before utilizing the tools that we recommend at this stage, you have to do a little bit of prework. First, remove duplicate ideas (i.e. "cross train staff", and "train all staff to do both tasks"). Second, utilize what we like to call a "common sense" filter. This is when you remove the ideas that are just not practical. Perhaps you know you can't hire new staff – get rid of the ideas that suggest that. Are some ideas aimed at adding resources or modifying things in a way that is just not possible? Does someone want to break down walls and build a new layout? If these things are truly not feasible due to project scope or constraints – then remove them now before moving on to the next phase. Have an open discussion with the team so that everyone knows why ideas are being removed from consideration. Lastly, ensure that each of the solutions is aimed at addressing one of the verified root causes. This is typically a quick check, but you want to make sure that all of your root causes are being addressed by an idea and that you aren't going to spend time implementing ideas that are not actually addressing your root causes.

Here is a quick reference list for determining if an idea should move to the next round for evaluation:

Successful solutions:
- Address a true root cause
- Have more support than resistance
- Benefit exceeds the cost and the risk
- Small changes that can result in large gains

Unsuccessful solutions:
- Address a defect but result in an adverse impact on customers (patients or staff)
- Conflict with the organization's strategy
- Benefit is clearly less than the cost
- Violate a regulatory or organizational requirement

After assessing ideas to make sure they meet the basic criteria for moving forward, you will want to further evaluate them and start to compare them to one another. There are two tools that can be helpful for this: a PICK chart and a solution selection matrix. Below are instructions for both tools. You will only need to do one with your team. The PICK chart is generally the favorite tool because it is simple for the team to understand and complete, but highly effective at determining which solutions will have the highest impact and require the least amount of effort. A solution selection matrix is a bit more mathematical (read: nerdy), but is really helpful when you have multiple solutions that you want to assess for impact on several criteria that are important. This is especially useful when evaluating software tools. For example, if you want to assess solutions for their impact on patient care, their impact on staff satisfaction, their overall ease of completion, their cost, and their change management needs – that might be a lot to think about in a PICK chart and thus better suited for the solution selection matrix. You can also do a solution selection matrix for things like picking your college, deciding between job offers, choosing a destination for your family vacation, and even deciding between candidates for a job posting. But we wouldn't possibly know people who have done those sorts of things – those people would just be way too organized and methodical (read: AWESOME) for us.

Tool: PICK Chart

PURPOSE: To systematically think about the effort and benefit associated with implementing brainstormed improvement ideas.

HOW TO COMPLETE:

1. Draw a PICK chart on a poster or whiteboard for the team. There should be four large boxes and two axes (see example).

2. Be sure to appropriately label the axes and the boxes according to the example: "benefit" on the left and "effort" on the bottom.

3. Have the team define "effort" – this could be cost, time to implement, resources, resistance, etc.

4. Have the team define "benefit" – this is typically a goal from the charter or elimination/mitigation of a specific root cause.

5. When facilitating this activity, focus on one improvement idea at a time and have the team discuss the benefit of each idea and the amount of effort that it would take to implement the idea.

6. Using the axes and the team conversation, place the improvement idea in the appropriate box.

7. Repeat this process until all improvement ideas are located in one of the four boxes.

Tips:

- All improvement ideas should be in one of the four boxes. Do not put improvement ideas "on the line" or in the middle; the discussion should result in a decision as to if the benefit and effort are low or high.

- PICK stands for possible, implement, challenge, and kibosh - all of which are quadrant labels. Try not to get hung up on the labels when evaluating ideas.

- Keep in mind that effort can be multiple factors. When thinking about effort it is possible to think about cost and time. As long as "effort" is defined up front, it can be whatever the team decides.

- The benefit should be related to the overall project goals. Think about the charter problem statement. While there may be a benefit to some ideas – is there an actual benefit to the ultimate goal?

Example:
Ophthalmology Clinic Flow

The team utilized a PICK Chart to assess solutions for their impact on cycle time and patient satisfaction as compared to time and feasibility to implement

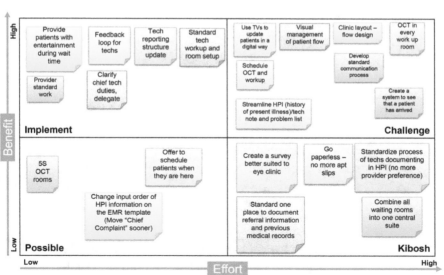

Tool: Solution Selection Matrix

PURPOSE: To prioritize and evaluate a variety of solutions that cannot all be implemented concurrently. This tool helps the user to weigh the impact of multiple solutions and compare those to the weight of other possible solutions.

PART ONE HOW TO COMPLETE:

The solution selection matrix should be done in two parts. Part one is creating operational definitions for each of the criteria elements. Each of the criteria will be given a rating of 1-5 for each proposed solution and it is important to make sure that they are all rated with the same criteria and operational definition.

1. First, create a list of the selection criteria to use.

2. Next, define what a rating of 1, 3, or 5 would look like for each of these criteria.

Part One Tips:

• When using the 1-5 rating, a 5 should always be the best and 1 should always be the worst rating. The recommended formula is designed to calculate the weighted ranking and the higher the number, the more impact associated with that solution.

• Determining the criteria and the operational definitions for each criteria should be decided as a team, even if part two is completed individually.

PART TWO HOW TO COMPLETE:

The second part of the Solution Selection Matrix is assigning weight to each criteria and each possible solution.

1. Using a format as shown in the example below, list each of the criteria from part one across the top.

2. Next, each criteria needs to be given a weight. This allows for criteria that are more important, to count for more in the final ranking than criteria that are less important. For weight, put in a percentage for each criteria. They should all total 100%.

3. Next, list each of the potential solutions vertically. Then, working across, assess each of the solutions for each of the criteria listed, giving each criteria a rating of 1-5 for that solution. Create a formula (see below) to calculate a ranking for each solution based on the weight of each criteria and the rating (1-5). This ranking can be compared among each of the potential solutions to determine which solutions will have the greatest impact.

Part Two Tips:

-   In order for this to work, you need to set up a formula in the "Ranking" column. The formula for this in Microsoft Excel would multiply each individual criteria score by the weight assigned for that criteria, and then add all of those values together. For the example shown, the formula looks like this: =B6*B$4+C6*C$4+D6*D$4+E6*E$4+F6*F$4

- Be sure to keep the rating for each criteria consistent — refer back to the chart created in part one frequently to ensure consistency.

- Think honestly about the weight assigned to each criteria — for instance, if cost is going to be a big concern, give cost a higher percentage of the weight than something like time to implement, which may not be something that would completely stop the presses.

- The second part of the solution selection matrix is great for the team to do together. However, if the team is one that might give varied feedback, it can be helpful to have each team member fill this out individually and then send to the project leader ahead of the meeting. The project leader can aggregate the responses and then discuss the final result with the team.

- The solution selection matrix is best used when there are a lot of solution ideas, when it isn't very clear which solutions should be implemented, or when there are a lot of pros and cons for remaining ideas.

Example:
Ophthalmology Clinic Flow

While the team used a PICK chart, we have also included the same solutions in a solution selection matrix so that you can see how the decisions might have been different with the use of a different tool.

Part One:

Metrics	Rating Values Description		
Selection Criteria	1 (not good)	3 (in between)	5 (good)
Impact on Improving Patient Satisfaction	No anticipated improvement	moderate improvement anticipated	significant improvement anticipated
Impact on Decreasing Cycle Time	No anticipated decrease	Might decrease cycle time	Expected to decrease cycle time
Cost to Implement	Large cost	Small cost	No cost
Time to Implement	more than 1 month to implement	less than 1 month to implement	immediate implementation possible
Change Management needed for Implementation	Buy-in for this solution will be a significant challenge	Buy-in for this solution will require some change management efforts	No anticipated buy-in challenges

Part Two:

	Solution Selection Matrix					
	Opthalmology Clinic Flow					
Weight for each metric (total to equal 100%)-->	25%	25%	20%	20%	10%	100%
Potential Solutions	Impact on Improving Patient Satisfaction	Impact on Decreasing Cycle Time	Cost to Implement	Time to Implement	Change Management needed for Implementation	Ranking
5S OCT rooms	4	4	5	5	4	4.4
Schedule OCT and workup	5	5	5	1	1	3.8
Provider standard work	3	5	5	2	3	3.7
Feedback loop for techs	3	3	5	4	3	3.6
Develop standard communication process	3	3	5	4	2	3.5
Change input order of HPI information on the EMR template (Move "Chief Complaint" sooner)	2	2	5	5	5	3.5
Streamline HPI (history of present illness)/tech note and problem list	2	3	5	4	3	3.35
Clinic layout – flow design	4	5	3	1	2	3.25
Standard tech workup and room setup	3	4	3	3	3	3.25
Provide patients with entertainment during wait time	3	1	3	5	5	3.1
Create a system to see that a patient has arrived	2	2	4	5	3	3.1
Offer to schedule patients when they are here	1	1	5	5	5	3
Standardize process of techs documenting in HPI (no more provider preference)	2	3	5	3	1	2.95
Use TVs to update patients in a digital way	3	1	4	3	5	2.9
Visual management of patient flow	2	4	3	2	4	2.9
Clarify chief tech duties, delegate	2	2	5	3	2	2.8
Tech reporting structure update	2	2	5	3	2	2.8
Go paperless – no more appointment slips	2	2	5	3	1	2.7
Standard one place to document referral information and previous medical records	1	1	5	4	4	2.7
OCT in every work up room	3	4	1	1	2	2.35
Combine all waiting rooms into one central suite	1	2	2	1	4	1.75
Create a survey better suited to eye clinic	1	1	3	1	1	1.4

TESTING SOLUTIONS

Now that you have narrowed down the list of possible solutions, you can focus on a couple to test out. It is really important to approach your solutions with the intention to test them and discard them if they are not effective. This is important for ensuring that the right solutions get implemented and for helping with change management. You can test out solutions in a few ways. If you have modeling or simulation software, you might be able to utilize that. You can do a mock walkthrough of a change to see how it might impact operations. But most commonly, you will likely need to complete a pilot or a PDSA of the change.

A pilot is when you take a proposed solution and you test it out on a small scale. If your solution is to change the way that you schedule patients, maybe you make that change for two or three providers first and see how it goes. This can help to identify problems with the solution that might need to be addressed before implementing on a larger scale. This also creates an opportunity to collect data with the change in place to see if it is having the intended impact. It makes the change more manageable in size, cost, time, and risk. Using the pilot approach can have a big impact on change management and create buy-in for the solution as staff feel like this is not necessarily a permanent change and understand that they will have the ability to give feedback and possibly help influence adjustments to the solutions.

The format used for a pilot is called a PDSA – this stands for Plan, Do, Study, Act. There is also a model out there called PDCA – Plan, Do, Check, Act. They do essentially the same thing (and have both been attributed to originating with Dr. Walter Shewhart). With a PDSA, you pilot your solution in a systematic and controlled way, so that you can adequately plan for, execute, and evaluate the results of the solution. Let's look at the questions to ask yourself and steps to take in each step of a PDSA.

Plan
- What solutions need to be piloted?
- Where will the pilots be conducted?
- How will the pilots be conducted?
- When and for how long will pilots run?
- Who will be involved in the pilot?
- How will the changes be communicated?
- What are the predicted outcomes of the pilot?
- What data will be collected?

Do
- Communicate the details about the pilot goals, plan, and timeline.

- Rally participants and ensure proper coverage.
- Perform quick training of staff.
- Execute the detailed PDSA plan, including data collection.
- Be present (please do not take a vacation during your pilot – we wouldn't say it, if we hadn't seen it).

Study
- Did the improvement meet project goals?
- Were the instructions clear, completed, and followed?
- What aids would have helped?
- What barriers/difficulties were encountered?
- Did the results match the prediction?
- How much was the gap between desired state and actual state reduced?
- Were the plans effective in addressing the root causes?
- Did you get any feedback from customers regarding the changes?
- Has enough progress been made or do you need to try other solutions?
- Were there unintended benefits or negative side effects?

Act
- Is another pilot needed or can we move to implementation?
- What lessons from the pilot should be applied to implementation?
- What are the risks to full implementation of this change?
- Are there any steps that need to be changed for a broader implementation or customized by department?

Following this format can help to evaluate the success of the solution before undergoing large efforts for a failed implementation. We have seen pilots that are immediately successful – both large and small gains. We have seen pilots that need to be tweaked along the way before getting to the right end product. And we have seen pilots that are failures right out of the gate. The key to evaluating a pilot is to give it a solid chance – if things aren't working, determine what can be changed or tweaked that might help to have a positive impact. But you also have to know when to give up on a solution and try one of the others on your list instead. There is nothing wrong with trying a solution and failing. That is part of learning and part of the process. That is why we pilot, so that we can fail on a smaller scale, recover quickly, and try the next thing. You'll never find the next great solution if you don't have a mindset that is open to failure. Do try not to get too flustered during the pilot. Be prepared to listen to feedback from staff, make adjustments on the fly, and watch for unintended consequences. It is important to be present, huddle with staff regularly, and continue to manage expectations throughout the pilot. If you have multiple solutions that you are going to test, you will likely want to conduct separate pilots unless some of them seem appropriate to combine and execute as one pilot.

After the pilot is complete, you will need to decide if you want to fully implement the solution, refine it and try again, or abandon it all together. Looking at the data from the pilot, you should compare new data visuals to those that you created in measure. Has there been a substantial change? If you really want to make your new Blackbelt friends happy, you'll even consider doing a hypothesis test to determine if there has been a statistically significant change in process performance. Even if the change isn't statistically significant (though there are serious bragging rights if it is!), a positive change is still fantastic and can help support fully implementing the solution.

Check out the tool below - a PDSA worksheet that can help you think through each step of a PDSA.

Tool: PDSA Worksheet

PURPOSE: To plan a PDSA cycle and capture observations and analysis of that cycle.

HOW TO COMPLETE:

1. Create a worksheet like the example and start by filling in the descriptive information related to the PDSA cycle.

    a. What are the beginning and end dates of the PDSA cycle? What is the objective of the PDSA? What does the team hope to accomplish?

2. Next, fill in the planning portion of the worksheet.

    a. What actions do the team plan to take for the PDSA cycle? What are the expectations or predications for the PDSA cycle?

    b. Identify what actions need to be taken during the PDSA cycle. This might include training, monitoring, check-ins with front line staff, etc. Assign someone who is responsible for completing these actions.

3. Once the PDSA cycle has been completed, fill in the remaining portions of the worksheet. For the "do" section, was the PDSA cycle carried out as planned and what were the observations?

4. Study the results of the PDSA. Did the results match the initial predictions? What was learned from the PDSA cycle? Were the goals of the PDSA cycle met?

5. Next, determine the next steps or actions as a result of the PDSA cycle. What can be concluded from this cycle? Is another cycle needed? If so, what modifications will the team make to additional cycles?

Tips:

- Remember that just because the PDSA cycle did not meet all of the expected goals, does not mean that it was a failure. Some elements of the cycle may have had a positive impact and additional alterations to a future cycle might help to achieve those goals.

Example:
Ophthalmology Clinic Flow

One of the pilots in Ophthalmology was creating a "pod" set-up what would co-locate workup technicians with the providers. This would allow the patients to move less during their visit and also would allow for better communication between the workup technicians and the providers.

PDSA Worksheet				
Project Title: Ophthalmology Clinic Flow		**Pilot Start:** 10/1		**Pilot Complete:** 10/30
What is the objective of the pilot? To decrease patient transportation in clinic and increase communication between staff				
PLAN		STUDY		
We plan to: Rearrange the location of providers and workup technicians in clinic to create pods based on subspeciality service		**Did the results match the prediction?** (Yes) No		
		What did we learn? We learned the value of a quick staff huddle and increased communication.		
Predicted results: Increase patient satisfaction, decreased wait time (due to better patient visibility for staff) and increased staff communication				
Steps Required	**Responsible**	**Did we meet our measurement goals?** We did not meet the goal for reducing patient wait time. Although some of their wait time was decreased, it is clear that there are other bottlenecks in the process that need to be addressed to fully reach the goal.		
Complete analysis of patient volumes per hour for each provider	Practice manager			
Obtain floor plan and determine which subspecialities should be located in each hallway	Practice manager and Lead techinician			
Notify technicians and providers of their new locations	Medical director	ACT		
Schedule daily huddles for each pod	Lead technician	**What did we conclude from this pilot?** We are going to keep this change but are also going to move forward with other pilots to continue to decrease patient wait time.		
Create standard room set-up and standard workup process	Three technicians			
DO				
Was the pilot carried out as planned? (Yes) No		**What action will occur as a result of the pilot?** Fully implement the change.		
What did we observe? Patients praised the new layout. Most staff were pleased with the new setup and many commented on better feedback from the providers regarding their workups. Providers appreciated the smoother flow.				

Example:
Pathway to Discharge

One pilot in the Pathway to Discharge project was to test the use of interdisciplinary discharge rounding (IDDR) on the units to determine if this resulted in earlier discharges.

Project Title: Pathway to Discharge – Interdisciplinary Discharge Rounding Pilot	Pilot Start: 5/5	Pilot Complete: 5/13

What is the objective of the pilot? To test out the utilization of IDDRs on surgical units to improve performance on discharge time of day

PLAN	STUDY
We plan to: Pilot using interdisciplinary discharge rounding (IDDR) on two surgical nursing units (1N & 3N).	**Did the results match the prediction?** Yes (No)
Predicted results: Move average discharge time of day to earlier in the day and increase patient and staff satisfaction with the discharge process and communication.	**What did we learn?** The time of day selected for IDDR on each unit may not be the optimal time for securing needed attendees. Some surgical provider teams may be more able to attend if there is an option to join by phone.

Steps Required	Responsible
Develop IDDR checklist	Team Activity
Engage and train proposed IDDR attendees (providers, nursing, care managers and physical therapy)	Blackbelt and Physician coach
Develop sheet for tracking IDDR attendance and impact	Care Manager
Select time for IDDR on each unit and secure conference rooms	Nursing Supervisor
Have team members assigned to help support IDDR during pilot	Team

Did we meet our measurement goals? No. We seem to clearly be in the learning curve for this intervention, not seeing a big shift in performance yet.

ACT

What did we conclude from this pilot? Care teams provided positive feedback on the IDDR approach. Believe it needs more time to integrate into daily operations.

DO

Was the pilot carried out as planned (Yes) No

What did we observe? Highly variable attendance at IDDR during week 1 of pilot. Teams needed support with the utilization of the IDDR checklist and the discussions seemed to be most valuable when all of the care team representatives were present.

What action will occur as a result of the pilot? Recommend adjusting IDDR times on each unit and continuing to pilot with team members joining to support IDDR on each unit.

IMPLEMENTING

Once you have found a solution that works and you make the decision to implement it on a larger scale, there are a few things to consider:

Review and modify team membership as appropriate

As you move into a full implementation, you may need to consider new team members if those being impacted by the change are not already on the team. Make sure you have adequate representation from staff who will be carrying out the implementation efforts.

Create an activity schedule and timeline

Determine how the implementation will be carried out. Will this be rolled out in phases? Will some changes occur prior to others? What training and standard work materials need to be created before the implementation can occur?

Determine Risks

Consider risks associated with implementing the solution. Develop contingency plans to prevent large scale disruptions to operations or any lapses in patient care. There are multiple tools available that might help to support this assessment.

Meet with the process owner and communicate the change

Ensure that the process owner (if that isn't you) is involved in the implementation plan and is prepared to be involved and take ownership of the process as implementation occurs. Communicate the change appropriately to all staff and stakeholders involved.

Just like everything else we've talked about, it can be helpful to have a plan! If you weren't expecting a plan, then you probably haven't been paying attention. If you want your implementation to be successful, you must plan accordingly. Below is a suggested template that can help you think through each change and action item to ensure the implementation goes smoothly.

Action date	Description of change	Action item	Who is responsible for implementing the change?	Data to collect	Who will collect the data?	Needs (tools/ training/ communication/ documentation)

If you have implemented solutions and are seeing positive results associated with those efforts, then you are ready to move on to the Control phase. The goal of Improve is to meet your project goals – only you, your sponsor, and your team can decide for sure if you have adequately met those goals or if further solutions are needed. Just like with the other phases, there are some questions that you can ask yourself and discuss with your sponsor to help ensure that you are ready to move to Control:

- Did you do benchmarking, implement Lean solutions, or generate new ideas?
- What criteria did you use to select the solutions to be tested?
- How did you test the proposed solutions and what were the results?
- Did you compare baseline performance to performance during the pilot? Was there an improvement?
- Did you test the improvement for statistical significance? (woohoo!!)
- Where do you see the potential for resistance going forward?

You are almost done with this book and your project! Let's walk through the Control phase and wrap this up!

Chapter Six:
Control

After all of the excitement of piloting your ideas in Improve, now you and your team are ready to move into Control. Control, in our experience, can be the most challenging phase of a DMAIC project (and honestly it's the least glamorous). The work of the Control phase is to take the improvements that made a big splash in Improve and put systems and structures in place to help those improvements become part of day-to-day operations. The really successful DMAIC projects are the ones where, after the control phase, the staff are no longer referring to that component of their workflow as part of "that project". The work has become part of the fabric of what they do and blends into daily operations.

It is not uncommon for your team, and for you as the improvement leader, to be running low on energy for your project coming into the Control phase. Improve is exciting (and hard work). You have been out and about supporting your pilots, measuring impact, and communicating status updates with stakeholders. Now that you know what your recommendations are for change, the work of preparing for handing off to operations begins.

In the Control phase the future state for your process becomes the new current state. We like to remind students at this point in their project work that it is not enough to put an effective solution in place – it must be maintained. What this requires for work by your improvement team is the development of a process for monitoring key measures, reviewing work methods, and taking appropriate actions when problems occur. In Control, there are several key components to discuss: standard work, communication and training, monitoring of ongoing performance, transition to operations, and summary and celebration. A key component of preparing for the transition to operations is the development and implementation of standard work, so let's start there.

STANDARD WORK

Standardization – what comes to mind when you say this word out loud? Some people have a negative gut reaction to the word standardization because they think it means everything needs to be exactly the same. But part of the goal of a DMAIC project is to reduce the variation in a process so that you can have more reliable outcomes for your patients and process customers. So, in the Lean Six Sigma world, standardization is your friend.

Standard work is the current best way to complete an activity or task with the proper outcome and the highest quality. A few things to note in this definition. The word "current" is not in there by accident. As a continuous improvement project leader, you have learned that there are always opportunities for improvement. The word current is in the definition to reflect this. The standard work developed today may evolve over months and years as the needs of the customer, the process, and/or the business change. Additionally, the word "best" is there to reinforce the fact that standard work is a key tool for the promotion and implementation of process standardization.

So you may be wondering what exactly is standard work? If you have ever utilized a procedure, checklist, job aid, workflow diagram, etc. then you are familiar with it. Standard work can go by many names and take on many forms – but they all have the same purpose – process standardization.

Some tips for developing standard work:

1. Include the staff that are or will be doing the work in the development process. The people doing the work will be best equipped to help document the new approach.
2. Solicit feedback on the best format. You don't want to waste your time developing a piece of standard work that is not in a format that is easily used or readily accessible to staff.
3. Avoid writing a novel. Sometimes teams get so excited about standard work (yes, this really happens!) that they try to write down absolutely everything in a standard work document. You can then end up with a lengthy document or binder that will gather dust and not be used by staff. Aim to be concise and limit yourself to focusing on items that will help set staff up for success.

Try utilizing the following process for developing standard work:

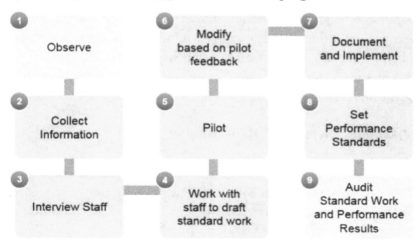

When developing standard work it is common to go through multiple iterations of the document or tool and test it until your team lands on the format and content that works best with staff. Don't let this bog you down – it is normal – and a sign that staff are engaged in helping to get it right.

A note of caution – standard work is not a cure-all. It does not suddenly make every process operate at a level of perfection. Natural process variation and human error do not disappear because you went through the effort of creating standard work. What it does do is help to reduce the likelihood of errors or defects because staff have access to the information they need, when they need it, and are set up for success in their daily work.

To ensure standard work is having the best impact it can, it is important that it is maintained and kept up to date. Developing a standard review cycle with your team will help to support this effort. Changes should not be made until there is data to show that a new alternative is better. Occasionally teams can get so excited by standard work that they are editing it constantly! This can have a negative impact of staff not trusting the documents because they are constantly changing. An audit step (leaders reviewing staffs' use of standard work) can also be helpful in maintaining it over time. Audits can be incorporated into leader rounding or staff huddles to help reinforce the adherence to the standard. The auditing process is helpful for uncovering barriers staff may face in adhering to the standard work and could provide information about opportunities for future revisions or training needs.

COMMUNICATION AND TRAINING

With your final recommendations for improvement coming out of the Improve phase and your standard work developed to support workflow changes, you are ready to launch into the communication and training component of the Control phase.

This should not be the first time in your project that you are sitting down to plan out communications and training for staff and leaders. However, at this point in the project work, you have moved from pilot planning and preparation to final implementation. Both your communication and training plans (a communication plan is addressed in the next chapter, if you'd like more details) should be robust and comprehensive to ensure that all stakeholders (think upstream and downstream of the impacted workflow) are well informed and trained.

For communications, you should tailor your messaging to stakeholders based on what each stakeholder group needs to know. Some stakeholders may just need basic awareness about the changes, others may need in-depth information to prepare appropriately for implementation.

There are a variety of communication methods you can choose to utilize: memos, emails, phone calls, in-person 1x1s, group meetings, town halls, etc. Most improvement leaders will end up utilizing a sampling of different communication approaches. A good rule of thumb is that the more someone's day-to-day work is going to be impacted by your team's recommended changes, the more frequent and in person your communication approach should be.

Could you imagine being on the receiving end of a major workflow change and the only communication you received about it was an email a few days before you go live? Yeah, we've all seen that. Make a choice right now to never do that to others. It's stressful for staff (and typically not a very successful approach anyway). A misstep like that could put a serious damper in the engagement and enthusiasm that you managed to drum up thus far.

When it comes to training, many of the same tips and recommendations apply. If you are really changing up someone's workflow – then your training approach should be more comprehensive and in person. Some different approaches to training include: policy and procedure review/sign-off, e-learning, classroom training, see one do one, simulation training and practice or super user training and support. When considering instructors for training approaches, your team members can be a great resource as they are well informed on the recommendations you are implementing as well as the improvement journey that they have been on. They can share what they have learned with staff that they are training, in addition to helping sell the positive impact of the changes.

MONITORING OF ONGOING PERFORMANCE

You have done a fantastic job of making improvements to a process. You have created standard work. You have communicated and trained appropriately. You have almost prepped everything for transition to the process owner. Now what? Now we have to make sure that we continue to track performance and that your process owner knows what to monitor going forward. This is where key performance indicators come in.

Key performance indicators are metrics that help to paint the picture of your process performance. KPIs come in two flavors: outcomes metrics and process metrics (sorry, no chocolate flavored KPIs. I bet you wish we really were talking about ice cream instead of math again, right?).

Outcome metrics provide insight into the output, or end result, of a process. Outcome metrics typically have an associated data-lag due to time passing before the outcome of a process is known. The primary outcome metric for a project is typically identified by project teams early on in their project work. It's the metric that your project sponsors are typically most interested in receiving updates on and that your team is most excited to share (likely one included on your charter). An example of an outcome metric would be a hospital acquired infection (HAI).

Process metrics, on the other hand, provide feedback on the performance of elements of the process, typically as it happens. It is common for process metrics to focus on the identified drivers of process performance. Process metrics can provide a preview of process performance for project teams and allow them to work proactively to address performance concerns. An example of a process metric related to HAI prevention is hand washing.

Thinking more about the example: if you were observing hand hygiene compliance on a nursing unit and and compliance was 65% for the day you observed, you could speak with the nurse manager of the unit and actions could be taken to enhance awareness about the importance of hand hygiene. Increasing hand hygiene compliance for that week could have a positive impact on reducing HAIs. That's the power of the process metrics – you get a heads-up on process performance and can take action to help support a better level of performance on your outcomes metrics. If you only look at the HAI data (the lagging outcome metric), it would be harder to take action on the specific drivers of that data.

Some examples of outcome and process metrics are included below to help you get a sense for the difference between the two.

Example	Process Metrics	Outcome Metrics
Football	• Rushing yards • Passing yards • # of turnovers • # of sacks • # of tackles	• Score of the game • Winner/loser
Clinic Flow	• Wait time in waiting room • Number of people in line • Length of exam • # of rooming staff that show up for work • Minutes past expected start	• Patient satisfaction scores • Percent on time • Average number of minutes past expected duration
LOS for stroke patients	• Minutes to treatment • Time between treatment and being ambulatory • Presence of an infection post surgery • Time between discharge order and discharge	• Length of stay • Readmission rates • Mortality rate

Some questions for project teams to consider when developing KPIs include:
- What does success look like?
- How will it be known if performance is trending away from goals?
- What data would the stakeholders and sponsors be most interested in?
- What data is available to the team?

Some tips for success when developing and selecting KPIs:

1. Select metrics that are meaningful to both the project team and the leaders and staff who will be monitoring the data. Take the time to solicit input on the KPI options from those close to the work.

2. Be realistic and select KPIs that can be rather easily measured. If a KPI requires an elaborate, time-consuming chart review and sampling process on a weekly basis to sustain it – question how realistic it is that someone would have the bandwidth to keep that review going. It is not uncommon for your data collection approaches to change from piloting to Control – so be open to new KPI opportunities.

3. Make sure you are selecting KPIs that are within your sphere of influence and control. Sometimes teams can get excited about creative metric ideas – but if they are beyond the scope of the project then the metric will not be meaningful to support process control.

A core tool of the Control phase is the control plan. The name pretty much says it all – this is the documentation of your team's plan for Control (this is the final, dare we say most important, plan of all – nah, they're all super important!). Your team should select three to six key performance indicators to recommend for monitoring long term to support process control. The control plan is one of the primary sources of information that will be utilized in the handoff of the project from the improvement team to the operational leader(s). This means that your process owner, if not on your project team already, should be pulled in and involved in the crafting of the Control Plan to set it up for success.

Tool: Control Plan

PURPOSE: To create a plan to sustain improvement made during the project.

HOW TO COMPLETE:

1. In a grid, or Excel spreadsheet, list three to six key performance indicators (KPI) to be monitored in the first column.

2. Then, work across the grid to fill in the following details about each KPI.

3. Determine how, where, and when the KPI will be measured.

   a. Operational Definition: indicate the specific definition that will be used to describe the metric.

   a. Measurement Source: EMR, other system, clinic observation, etc.

   a. Measurement Frequency: How frequently? Monthly, weekly, etc.

4. Determine the standard to which the performance will be measured against. It might help to look at the project goals and accomplishments for this. If the goal was to schedule all new appointments within 3 days and you achieved that during Improve, then 3 days would probably be the standard.

5. Next determine who analyzes the data, who acts on the data, and what that action looks like.

a. Who Analyzes: This is the person responsible for checking the data against the standard, running the reports, and doing any manual data collection.

b. Who Acts: This is the person who is notified when performance is not aligned with the standard and who completes the predetermined action steps.

c. What is Done when Standard is Not Met: This is the sequence of actions that happens when current performance does not meet the standard. For example, if new appointments are taking 5 days to schedule, what is the action to follow up on that?

Tips:

- Think about the critical control variables that can be monitored to ensure that gains from the project are sustained over time. Focus on variables that can easily be measured without too much manual data collection.

- The more automated the review of this data, the better the chance of process owners continuing to monitor the data. Try to be realistic about the frequency with which each variable needs to be tracked for compliance.

- Many times the first action might be to dive deeper into the data or do more research to understand what caused the standard to not be met. It is important to understand the reason for the deviation from the standard before one can apply any definitive action. Remember the importance of recognizing if the variation is special or common cause before acting!

- The control plan is a document for the process owner. If the process owner is different from the project leader, it is important for the two parties to sit down and discuss the control plan together to ensure it is agreed upon.

- A project leader can create a great control plan, but it will not be useful if the process owner does not understand it or agree with some of the indicated fields.

- When filling in who is responsible for analyzing and acting on the data, use titles or roles as opposed to individual names. This is important as positions have turnover to ensure that everyone knows who is responsible for each item.

- Identify only the necessary variables needed to ensure control of the new current state – this does not need to include every variable that was measured during the project.

Example:
Ophthalmology Clinic Flow

The Ophthalmology project team worked collaboratively to develop the control plan below. The process owners provided information on what data was easiest for them to access and what frequency of review seemed most appropriate for monitoring.

Key Performance Indicator (KPI)	How Measured	Where Measured	When Measured	Standard	Who Analyzes	Who Acts	What Is Done When Standard Is Not Met
Average Workup Time	Workup Completed minus Workup Start for Follow-up Patient Visit Type (hh:mm:ss)	Ophthalmic Events Data	Weekly	< 22 min	Business Manager	Clinical Supervisor & Business Manager	* Review data by technician and by provider (stratify) * Look at the weeks that are meeting the goal and understand causes for variation in performance * Rounding on technicians if individual feedback is required * Addressing scheduling or systems issues in collaboration with staff
Imaging Wait Time	Imaging Start minus Workup Completed for patients that received imaging (hh:mm:ss)	Ophthalmic Events Data	Weekly	< 15 min	Business Manager	Clinical Supervisor & Business Manager	* Review the patient schedule and imaging staffing for the week * Review details to see if we had a number of patients arrive at the same time
Total Visit Cycle Time	Provider Complete minus Patient Check In time (hh:mm:ss)	Ophthalmic Events Data	Weekly	< 100 min for Retina	Business Manager	Clinical Supervisor & Business Manager	* Review the patient schedule and imaging staffing for the week * Review details to determine any Retina specific issues leading to delays
Patient Experience Wait Times	Wait time at Clinic (from arriving to leaving) (% Top Box)	Patient Experience Survey Data	Monthly (data lag)	> 60%	Business Manager	Leadership Team	* Support staff in updating patients * Share patient comments with Staff * Incorporate follow-up into staff meetings
Patient Experience Delay/ Wait Time Communication	Degree to which you were informed about any delays (% Top Box)	Patient Experience Survey Data	Monthly (data lag)	> 60%	Business Manager	Leadership Team	* Support staff in updating patients * Share patient comments with Staff * Incorporate follow-up into staff meetings

Example:
Pathway to Discharge

In order to show you the variety in control plan metrics and actions, we have also included the control plan for the Pathway to Discharge project.

KPI	How Measured	Where Measured	When Measured	Standard	Who Analyzes	Who Acts	What Is Done When Standard Is Not Met
Average Discharge Time of Day by Unit	Average of discharge time of day for patients discharged from unit	EMR	Weekly	< 1:00 PM	Analyst	Nursing Unit Leadership	* Stratify data by surgical service, analyze for trends * Review sample of late discharges to identify issues leading to late discharge
Patient Satisfaction with speed of discharge (% Top Box Scores)	Patient Experience Surveys	Reporting Tool	Monthly	> 70% Top Box Scores	Analyst	Nurse Manager	* Review patient comments * Utilize volunteers to ask patients questions based on findings to learn more
% of Discharge Orders Signed by 10:00 AM	# orders signed by 10:00 AM / Total Discharge Orders	EMR	Weekly	> 40% Signed by 10:00 AM	Analyst	Medical Directors	* Review data by surgical service, stratify by provider * Medical director to round on providers with low % to support timely discharge orders
Attendance at IDDR by Service (%)	# of staff attending/ # of staff expected	Manual tracking log	Daily	> 95% attendance	Care Manager	Nurse Manager and Provider Coach	* Review attendance log, for consistent attendance issues with no note explaining cause (i.e. conference attendance, time away etc.) reach out to care team to determine barriers to attendance
30 Day All Cause Readmissions (%)	# of patients readmitted within 30 days/total # of discharges	EMR	Monthly	Maintain < 6%	Analyst	Nursing Unit Leadership	* Balancing metric, if noticing performance trending higher than expected stratify data and discuss with leadership team

It is important to touch on data visualizations and control charts once more. You learned about the nitty gritty on control charts back in the Measure phase. Control charts (as the name implies) are a handy tool for visualizing process control. We encourage project teams to utilize control charts for monitoring the project KPIs on their control plan, as this approach can help to readily identify and distinguish the difference between common cause and special cause variation.

In the Control phase, as performance on your KPIs is evolving, there may be an opportunity to spilt or change your control limits to reflect the shift in performance. The statistical signal for a need to split control limits would be when there is evidence of a shift (7 or more points in a row on the same side of the mean). Note that control limits should only be split if the change is intended to be permanent. The rule is that 24 data points are needed to accurately calculate control limits, so new limits would be considered "temporary control limits" until 24 data points (after the start of the shift) are collected. It can be helpful to annotate your control chart to label where process changes occurred. This helps to highlight the impact of your team's work.

Take a look at the control chart for the Ophthalmology Clinic Flow Project. You can see where the process improvements occurred and the impact that this had on reducing visit cycle time for the Retina service.

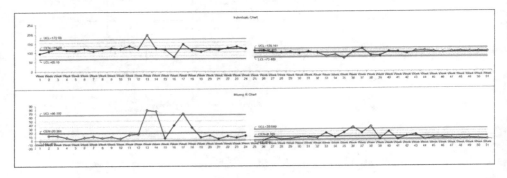

Control charts are just one of the options for visualization of your team's KPIs in Control. Below are some additional options for helping to support your control plan with creative tracking and socialization of your data.

Dashboards	• Provide visualization of multiple metrics in a graphical summary format. • Typically real-time data, refreshed frequently and available electronically.
Scorecards	• Provide clear performance variance from target information at a glance for your KPIs. • Typically updated at least monthly and posted on a data wall. May also be available electronically.
Control Charts	• Tracking your KPIs in the control chart format allows for visualization of process stability and special cause indicators. • Can be posted on a data wall and is updated based on the frequency of review assigned for each KPI.
Interactive	• You can also work with your team to get creative on how you are tracking your KPI performance over time. • Utilize visual analogies (football field, garden, etc.) to track progress on your data wall. • Make a game or competition out of achieving performance targets. • Have staff and team members involved in data collection and posting.

When considering data tracking and display options, it's a great opportunity to get team members and staff involved in the development of the approach. The more staff feel ownership of data and performance the more likely you are to see your results moving in the right direction. When people understand the 'why' for the work they do it can be a powerful motivator of performance. We encourage you to think creatively about how to share data or how to get staff excited about data. In a project led by one of us, staff had a poster with a "pot of gold" picture for each day. Every time that they completed a new patient referral, they placed a sticker in the pot. This allowed them to see how they were doing from day-to-day, and also gave them a little satisfaction each time they added a sticker to the pot. Leadership was excited to see this display and ended up offering small rewards when they saw overflowing pots.

TRANSITION TO OPERATIONS

The control phase represents a key handoff point in your DMAIC project. At this point in the project the improvement leader is passing the baton to the process owner to take the lead on seeing that the recommendations of the project are not only fully implemented but also sustained. Throughout the lifecycle of a typical DMAIC improvement project, the project effort and accountability for success slowly shifts from the project leader to the process owner. By the time you get to Control, the process owner becomes primarily responsible for the ongoing success of the project work. A visual of this shift is shown below for context.

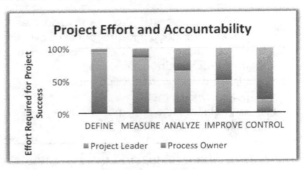

As the improvement leader, your work to prep for this handoff is focused on how you can set the process owner up for success. Much of what we have discussed in Control up to this point has prepped you for this handoff. You have documented workflow changes in your standard work and collaborated with the process owner around the communication and training approach for the implementation of the new standard work. You and your team selected meaningful and measureable KPIs that the process owner feels comfortable supporting long term. You have worked collaboratively with the process owner to draft a control plan that will be utilized to monitor process performance moving forward.

Note that preparing the process owner for this handoff may involve some training for the process owner. It is not uncommon for the project leader to spend time with the process owner going over the control plan in detail, and even practicing to pull data from a reporting tool and visualize it in a control chart or other format. There could also be an opportunity to create standard work for the process owner on how to execute on the control plan.

The handoff to the process owner should be a formal step in your project closure. Set up a meeting with the process owner to walk through the components of the control plan and cover all of the remaining items – any odds and ends – that you have wrapped up as an improvement leader. Then literally hand-off the project by handing the process owner your documentation package (you can do this document handoff electronically too for ease of future use).

Completing the handoff does not mean that you won't answer emails and phone calls from the process owner – but simply that you will not be there for the day to day work of supporting Control. (Unless you are the process owner, then there is no getting out of it! – and this handoff section could have been skimmed).

SUMMARIZE AND CELEBRATE

No project is complete until you have celebrated! Before you bust out the champagne (or more likely, sparkling cider – this is a work place, after all), consider one last tool, the storyboard. A storyboard poster is a great way to pull together all of the work your improvement team has completed over the course of your DMAIC journey and put it in one place. This may seem like an unnecessary step – but trust us – having a poster highlighting your team's work will come in handy.

Storyboard posters can be utilized and posted in the department that completed that work to celebrate success and remind staff of the reason for the changes in their workflow. They can also be utilized to socialize and spread your improvement work and ideas to other areas. Additionally, project teams can submit their completed project work and posters to local, regional, and/or national conferences for a professional development opportunity.

Some tips for storyboards:

1. Keep it visual
2. Keep it concise
3. Make it easy to follow the story (don't assume the knowledge of the audience)

An example of a storyboard one of our students completed at Dartmouth-Hitchcock is shown below. This storyboard looks at the process of optimizing the flu vaccination clinic. Even with no prior knowledge of the project, you can follow the storyboard and get a clear understanding of the project work.

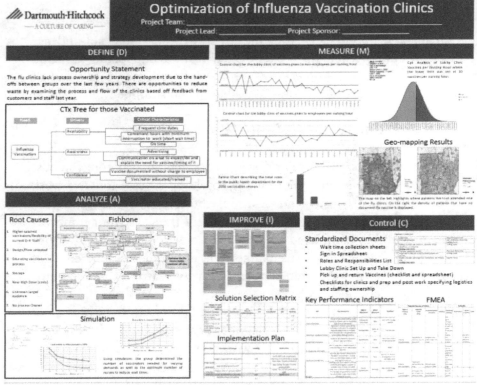

There are lots of opportunities for variety in the format and content. The storyboard framework comes with a lot of creative flexibility – we encourage your teams to take advantage of that! Share your DMAIC journey with pride and creative flare.

Lastly, we encourage you to recognize your team for the time and effort they have contributed to the project in a way that would be meaningful to them. You typically have gotten to know your team well by now and may have some great ideas for recognition. However, if you find yourself stumped on what they might like – just ask! Remember back in Define we talked about the Voice of the Customer? Here's a chance to practice!

Some ideas for celebration and recognition that we have seen go over well with teams include:

- Food – bringing in a treat or going out together for a meal
- Memento connected to the work of the team (symbolic)
- Senior leaders or operational leaders can send handwritten 'thank you' notes to team members
- Presentation opportunities to the department or organization
- Submitting project work to poster fairs or conferences
- Writing up the project work and submitting for publication

Project Updates

I bet you are wondering what happened with the Ophthalmology Clinic Flow and Pathway to Discharge projects weren't you? We have included a brief synopsis of the conclusion of these projects below to satisfy your curiosity.

OPHTHALMOLOGY CLINIC FLOW PROJECT

The team implemented a number of changes in the clinic including:
1. Standardizing exam room set up
2. Creation of a pooled or 'POD' model for technician assignments
3. 5S of the Imaging Suite
4. Customer service training for all technicians

The team also made recommendations regarding changes to the master schedule template and patient communication, but there wasn't enough support to move them forward at the time of project closure. The team's work made a statistically significant reduction in the visit cycle time for Retina patients, imaging wait times were trending down, and patient experience scores were trending up at time of closure. The improvement leader developed a monthly dashboard with control charts (along with standard work for updating it) and trained the process owner so that data can be shared with the leadership team and staff monthly for ongoing monitoring.

PATHWAY TO DISCHARGE PROJECT

The team had two primary interventions implemented including:

1. Interdisciplinary daily discharge (IDDR) rounds
2. Pre-Surgical Discharge Planning Questionnaire

The IDDR rounds were well received and the clinical teams with the most consistent attendance were starting to see some patients able to leave the hospital earlier in the day. At time of project closure the work of the team led to a statistically significant reduction in discharge time of day on one of the nursing units. The work did not negatively impact patient experience or readmissions. Project sponsors were provided with a comprehensive monthly data update for 18 months post project close. Since closure of the project, IDDRs have spread to additional units in the hospital.

Just like with each of the other phases, there are some key questions to answer in the Control phase:

- Has the process been appropriately transitioned into operations?
- Is there a plan in place to monitor ongoing performance and make adjustments as needed? Is someone accountable for this?
- Have roles and responsibilities been clearly defined?
- Did you take the time to recognize and celebrate your team for their efforts?

If you answered "no" to any of the questions above, then you are not quite done with your work. You cannot pass 'Go' and collect. You will need to circle back to finalize the answers to these questions with your team and process owner so you can get back to celebrating (and monitoring your KPIs of course!)

This marks the end of your DMAIC journey – but not the end of the book just yet. In the next chapter we will be sharing a selection of change management tools with you that we have found to be helpful in setting our students up for success over the years.

Chapter Seven:
Change Management

Welcome to the seventh and final chapter. You made it all the way through DMAIC! Woohoo! This is the part where we have to tell you that as fantastic as this process is, you sometimes need more than just the tools and the process to be successful. Every problem that you encounter, every process that you aim to improve, is going to involve people. People are essential to work processes. People bring passion and joy for their work, they bring commitment, and people are also difficult. Diverse perspectives in the workplace can be wonderful for sparking new ideas, viewing a process through a different lens, and embarking on great improvement efforts. Diverse perspectives can also be the pitfall of an entire project without proper communication and management of people going through the change.

Some projects can be smooth sailing. If you have an engaged sponsor, project team, and staff who do the work, sometimes change management needs are minimal. More frequently, minor to moderate change management is necessary for project success. I'm sure you've heard that change is hard, most people are aware of this. It is rare that all stakeholders have the same vision for improving a process. Even if all stakeholders agree on the destination, they will likely have different preferences and comfort zones for getting there. This is why it is helpful to have a toolkit that includes not just technical tools from the DMAIC framework, but also tools meant to help assess your environment and come up with actions to mitigate change management barriers. We are taking you beyond DMAIC, beyond Lean, into another dimension, called The Change Management Zone (Twilight Zone anyone? If you missed it – read it again with a sinister voice).

While we know how much you loved learning about the two projects we've used throughout the book, I am sorry to say that we will not be using those projects for the examples in this chapter. Change management needs vary from project to project, so we will be taking examples from projects that warranted using these tools and giving you the background information necessary to understand how each tool was used. You may find yourself referencing this chapter a lot when working on your project, or very little. It truly depends on how much change management is necessary. Regardless, there are also some tips for each DMAIC phase and the common change management moments we typically encounter. Sometimes just acknowledging that people might be uncomfortable with an aspect of the work will make a big difference in their engagement. Lastly, no matter how awesome we are at explaining change management issues that we've seen, we could never substitute for your sponsor (unless you are having challenges with your sponsor, then keep reading – and find a new sponsor!). If you are truly encountering change management issues that go above and beyond what the tools in this chapter can help with, you need to have a conversation with your sponsor. The commitment and support for a project and the project outcomes must be in place to ensure success. If you feel like you don't have that, talk to your sponsor about what you need and seriously consider if this is the right time for the project to move forward.

CHANGE MANAGEMENT CONSIDERATIONS BY PHASE	
Define	• Selling your project – convincing people it is important • Engaging stakeholders • Recruiting the team • Agreeing on a problem and scope
Measure	• Data collection – engage the project team and staff outside of the project team • Share data with operational staff and listen to their feedback • Share the flowchart and ask for feedback • Be ready to listen to questions or explanations about data – share insights humbly and follow up on suggestions or questions of others
Analyze	• Keep stakeholders informed of new information • Stay focused and don't let the team jump to Improve • Respect the people doing the work • Question current state with humble inquiry • Listen to concerns • Focus on the work or process, not the people
Improve	• Reactions to piloting – be prepared to listen and amend pilots as needed • Resistance to the new process • Get a commitment to try (This is key!) • Remind staff that nothing is written in stone, a PDSA is just an experiment
Control	• Handoff to the process owner • Training and communication with staff • Recognize contributions of team members • Use engaged staff as champions to maintain the work

The tools that we are going to walk through can be used solely for planning and assessment purposes – to help you understand where your stakeholders are at in regard to your project, and what challenges you might encounter. They can also be used as a foundation for taking action. None of them are a magic bullet. If you have change management barriers, you won't pull out one of these tools and watch the barriers disintegrate. They are meant to help you assess, plan, and understand. The actions that you take as a result of these tools are up to you, and those actions are what will help manage change throughout your project.

While we are going to start with a communication plan, it might also be helpful to do some type of stakeholder analysis at the beginning of your project. There are many tools and frameworks available that can help support you in better understanding how committed to the project your stakeholders are.

The communication plan is a tool that you can utilize throughout your project to help support effective communications with your project team and the groups of stakeholders that you identify. Referring back to the SIPOC (for that list of stakeholders) can be helpful when preparing to draft your communications plan.

The communication plan template we share is one that you can use, or if your organization has another format that is preferred, that works too. What's important, no matter what format it is in, is that you include the who, what, when and how in your communication plan.

Tool: Communication Plan

PURPOSE: To organize project communication details for all stakeholders impacted by the project.

HOW TO COMPLETE:

1. Start by listing out all of your key stakeholder groups.

2. Work with your team to identify what information needs to be communicated to each stakeholder group. The information could be called out specifically in your plan or generalized – for example, sharing a proj-

ect status update or distributing meeting minutes.

3. The plan should also include recommendations on when the information will be communicated and what method of communication will be utilized. Your communication method should be tailored to the stakeholder audience. Depending on the sensitivity of the communication or if you anticipate a higher resistance to change, you should plan for more frequent and in-person communication to provide stakeholders the opportunity to engage on the topic and for you to hear them out and develop change management tactics based on the needs of the stakeholders.

4. The last item in the communication plan is who will be delivering the message – in other words, the person sending the email, leading a Q&A session, or presenting the information.

Tips:

- Who delivers the communications does not need, and should not in most cases, always be the project leader. Incorporating multiple stakeholders into the role of message sender can be a valuable way to show the base of support for the work and the commitment of the team.

- Treat your communication plan as a living document, it should be utilized in all phases of your DMAIC project work (not just at the beginning or the end!)

Example:
Schedule Revision

We have included a communication plan example below for your reference, but again, this is only a suggested format and you can customize it or utilize other formats that meet the communication needs for your project. This communication plan was drafted for a project aimed at evaluation opportunities to revise a master schedule in a specialty clinic. This communication plan was drafted at the beginning of the project to ensure all key stakeholders were well informed and had an opportunity to provide feedback on the project charter.

	Stakeholders/Audience: The people or groups of people that should receive the information	When: Date of communication	Information to be Communicated (presentations, status report, project update, minutes, etc.)	How will the information be delivered? (email, meeting, etc.)	Message Sender: Name of the person or group that will provide the information
1	Department Chair	Sept 5th	Project charter review & feedback	Meeting with Greenbelt and Coach	Greenbelt
2	Medical Director	Sept 6th	Project charter review & feedback	Meeting with Greenbelt and Coach	Greenbelt
3	Leadership	Sept 7th	Project charter review & feedback	Meeting with Greenbelt and Coach	Greenbelt
4	All Dept. Staff	Monthly	Status updates	Email/Memo	Greenbelt
5	MA & Nursing Staff	Sept 19th	Project charter and voice of customer data collection	Staff meeting	Nurse Manager
6	MDs and APs	Sept 20th	Project charter and voice of customer introduction	Provider meeting & 1:1 follow-up to complete VOC	Greenbelt and Medical Director

Another planning tool that can be helpful to consider for your project is a RACI chart. A RACI falls under the larger umbrella of responsibility matrix tools. We have used RACI charts in two different ways. First, you can use a RACI chart to help delineate roles and responsibilities for the project work itself. Second, you can use a RACI chart to help delineate roles and responsibilities for a new process designed in the Improve phase, to ensure all stakeholders are on the same page. Either way, a RACI is a simple tool that can be very useful in setting boundaries and guidelines for expectations. Like with any document of this nature, it should be referenced as needed and enforced for maximum benefit.

Tool: RACI Chart

PURPOSE: To clearly identify the roles and responsibilities of team members and/or stakeholders as it pertains to a specific task or project.

HOW TO COMPLETE:

1. Start by listing all of the individual project tasks in the left-hand column. Then, horizontally along the top, list an individual or stakeholder group for each column.

2. Working down the list of tasks, look at each task and determine each person or stakeholder's role in that task. Is the person accountable, responsible, consulted, or informed for this task?

3. Continue down the list until all boxes have been filled in or intentionally left blank.

Tips:

- Be consistent with your definitions for each of the four categories, consider these:
  - Responsible: performs the work
  - Accountable: accountable for making sure the work gets done
  - Consulted: has information necessary to do the work
  - Informed: notified when the work is complete

- The accountable person may or may not be the person actually doing the work. However, he/she owns the work and would be the one experiencing the consequences for work that is not completed.

- The RACI chart is useful in helping to clear up any present role confusion and also to help avoid future role confusion as a project progresses.

- Oftentimes the project leader is the accountable person, however, this may not always be the case. It is possible for a sponsor or a process owner to also be the accountable person, so think through each task individually.

- There should only be one "A" per row – only one person accountable for each task. This helps to ensure clarity around the task.

- It is okay to have multiple "R"s in a row as multiple people may be working on the task.

- Some people may have multiple letters for the same task. It is possible to be both informed and accountable or to be both responsible and accountable.

- There may be some blank boxes on the chart if someone is not involved in a specific task at all.

- Review the chart and if one person seems to be responsible for many tasks, reevaluate to see if they are still the appropriate person for all tasks and if they have the bandwidth to complete them.

Example:
Schedule Optimization

A project focused on increasing patient throughput in an outpatient clinic identified the root cause of the problem of low patient throughput to be related to the current scheduling templates. Templates were created for individual providers with a lack of visibility to the clinic and clinic resources as a whole. One of the suggested improvements was to implement a new scheduling template that would take into account all shared resources within the department. This change resulted in a heavy lift for the clinic staff and a RACI chart was created to help understand who was involved in each step of the implementation plan.

Assignment/Task	Secretaries	Providers	Administrative Manager	Practice Manager	Physician Leader
Create scheduling templates that maximize clinic resources	C	C	R	A	I
Discuss changes with providers		C		A	R
Train staff on new scheduling templates	C		R	A	I
Create rules for maintaining template and capacity rules	C	C	R	A	C
Create plan for onboarding new providers within existing templates			C	R	A

Sometimes it is helpful to think about those first two tools as action tools and the rest as assessment tools. The following tools can be used to reflect on your resiliency as a project leader and assess the change management environment; there is no immediate or required action as a result. Action can always occur (and often probably should), but you can also use them to get a general lay of the land. For each of the tools that we describe next, consider whether or not it makes sense to do them with your team or solo. Sometimes doing them solo and then sharing them with your team for feedback is a good balance. If your team is open to talking honestly about the environment, then getting team members to participate can be really helpful when it comes time for the project team to take action as a result of the assessments. If you have a lot of interpersonal conflict on the team, or within the department, that isn't necessarily public, consider doing these tools alone and using the results to guide you and your work as an improvement leader through the project.

This first tool is meant to be utilized as a self-reflection tool for you as a project leader, typically prior to project kick-off or shortly thereafter. Every improvement project you lead presents an opportunity for learning, growth, and development of your skills utilizing DMAIC tools and leading teams (the people side of improvement work). With the busy business of preparing to kick-off a project, this tool may not get used frequently – or you may think, "Wow, I do not have time for reflection." But, as a leader, we encourage you to take a few minutes for yourself and either utilize this checklist or another reflection method or approach to help support your learning and development journey.

Tool: Resiliency Checklist

PURPOSE: To provide a framework for improvement leaders to reflect on the frequency of certain behaviors they do related to project leadership, communication, and support. This is an individual activity.

HOW TO COMPLETE:

1. Review each statement and then rate yourself on each behavior.

   The scale is:
   1 = Never,   2 = Occasionally,
   3 = Sometimes,   4 = Frequently,
   5 = Always

2. After completing your ratings, review statements where you rated yourself high or low and consider how your responses may impact your approach to your current project.

$\mathcal{T}$ips:

- Utilize your network – mentors, coaches, sponsors, etc. to seek out feedback and support for development in any growth areas you identify.
- Complete resiliency checklists at the beginning of each improvement project you do. Keep them to refer back to and enhance reflection on your growth and development as an improvement leader over time.

Example:

Schedule Optimization

An experienced improvement leader completed the resiliency checklist for a registration optimization project when preparing to kick off. Reflecting on the answers, an opportunity was identified to be more flexible and adaptable when changes occur.

Rate Behaviors
(1=Never, 2=Occasionally, 3-=Sometimes, 4=Frequently, 5=Always)

I know my own strengths and weaknesses and how that affects my role in the project	4
When I get discouraged, I ask for help and look for new opportunities to learn	3
I feel confident about my improvements skills	5
I anticipate project issues and am proactive in resolving these issues	4
I am interpersonally competent (am able to resolve issues among team members, manage the expectations of stakeholders, communicate progress)	4
I am passionate about the project	5
When problems or disruptions occur, I stay focused on the longer-term goals	3
I maintain communication and a clear direction for the project	4
When changes occur, I am adaptable and flexible	2

Now that we've taken some time to reflect as an improvement leader, let's learn about some tools that can help us assess our environment and its readiness for change. The SWOT is a great tool to start to identify the strengths and weaknesses of moving forward with a certain solution.

Tool: SWOT Analysis

PURPOSE: To help identify strengths, weaknesses, opportunities, or threats to an organization, department, project initiative, or other business venture. This helps to inform the strategy to use moving forward.

HOW TO COMPLETE:

1. Start by looking at strengths of the project or initiative. What prior experiences, resources, and current state factors are in the project's favor?

    a. Enthusiasm about change, unutilized staff capacity, etc.

2. Second, evaluate weakness for the project or initiative. In what areas is the project vulnerable?

    a. Lack of experience, poor morale in the department, inadequate resources, etc.

3. Now, focus thinking on the environment (external to the project or initiative itself). What opportunities exist that can be capitalized on?

    a. Grant funding, a developing culture of change, a promise of support from leadership, etc.

4. Finally, with the same focus on the environment external to the project, think about threats. Are there active or upcoming impediments to the work?

   a. A key staff member leaving, a new EMR implementation, a major change to a workflow, etc.

Tips:

- Try focusing on one quadrant at a time and capturing all thoughts and ideas before moving to another quadrant – focused thinking can help to capture more ideas.

- Strengths and weaknesses should be focused on internal factors (to the project or organization being evaluated). Opportunities and threats are focused externally on the environment (i.e. a new Joint Commission regulation would belong in opportunities or threats).

- This is a great brainstorming activity to do with team members and may be something to discuss with the project sponsor depending on how items balance out.

Example:
External Lab Resulting

A project focused on improving the workflow associated with external lab resulting in the EMR used a SWOT analysis to assess a possible solution. The problem addressed in this project was that providers would order lab tests, a patient would get those labs done at an external facility, and then the ordering provider would not receive notification of the lab results in any consistent or timely manner. This presented a problem when patients had results that required action. One solution that the team wanted to test was to have a centrally located staff member in the medical records department who would receive all incoming lab results and input them into the medical record in a standard way, then notify the appropriate provider that the results were available for review. As this was a big change that would result in needing to justify additional resources, we completed a SWOT to assess the solution during the pilot. The opportunities and threats were focused on the external lab facilities, and the strengths and weaknesses were focused on the new internal process. This SWOT allowed us to discuss the benefits of the new process as well as some existing concerns with the project sponsors.

Strengths	Weaknesses
• The medical records staff member is processing all lab results consistently and accurately. • Providers are pleased to receive all lab information in the same format and in a timely manner • All labs are being entered into the system within 24 hours of receipt (this was not trackable with the old process)	• The medical records staff member is not clinically trained and this could present a challenge without proper on-the-job training • If additional departments will want this service, additional staff will be required

Opportunities	Threats
• There is an opportunity to further educate external facilities on the new process to prevent them from sending results to medical records and the department directly	• Departments are still receiving lab results directly – these could be new or duplicate results. This could lead to confusion or labs received in the department being overlooked.

The losses and gains chart is a tool that can help you to assess how people might react to the change you wish to implement. Similar to the Goldratt Change Matrix, this tool is used to determine the pros and cons for changing or not changing, and also to create tactics that will support your change management efforts.

Tool: Losses and Gains Chart

PURPOSE: To understand the impact that specific changes will have on people and identify the ways to decrease resistance and increase commitment.

HOW TO COMPLETE:

1. Identify the stakeholder group being assessed and describe the current perspective of that group.

2. Identify specific losses and gains for that stakeholder group if the change occurs and if things remain the same.

   a. Focus on the perspective of the stakeholder group. What do they see as potential losses and gains? This may not be the same as what the team views as potential losses and gains.

3. Using the list of losses and gains, identify specific actions or tactics to address the stakeholder group.

4. Complete additional charts for other stakeholder groups as needed.

Tips:

- This chart might not be necessary for all stake-holder groups. If there are some groups who are already onboard with the change, it is likely not necessary to plan specific intervention tactics.

- This activity might not be appropriate to do with the team if any of the team members are resistant stakeholders. Think carefully about the team before deciding if this should be completed alone or as a group activity.

  - In many cases it can be helpful to complete this with the team, if the team members are engaged and can help identify those resistance points for other stakeholders not on the team (i.e. a very engaged secretary on the team might be able to help identify specific losses and gains from a secretary perspective and help come up with tactics for addressing his/her peers).

Example:
Referral Turnaround Time

In a project aimed at reducing the time it took to reschedule outpatient referrals in a clinic, we utilized a losses and gains chart to assess how the department secretaries would feel about the change in workflow. Root causes for the long length of time to schedule referrals were related to lack of ownership and lack of a standard process for scheduling referrals. The proposed change was to implement a standard workflow for processing referrals and to create a schedule that rotated responsibility for working new referrals and following up on old referrals each day of the week. The losses and gains chart helped us to identify secretarial concerns and brainstorm tactics for ensuring a successful pilot.

	+	-	Tactics
	Gains from the change	**Losses from the change**	**Maximize gains and minimize losses**
Change	Secretaries will feel less overwhelmed with figuring out where in the process an existing referral is	Secretaries will be required to work on referrals at times when they might prefer to complete other tasks	Create reference and training materials to ensure all secretaries have access to the information necessary to schedule appropriately
	All secretaries will work on referrals in the same manner, reducing the current variation in scheduling practices	Secretaries who are not as skilled at processing referrals will now be required to work on them	Set team goals for scheduling referrals to help secretaries embrace teamwork and stop viewing referrals as an individual burden or responsibility
	Secretaries will all share in the responsibility of referrals, reducing the feeling that a few secretaries are primarly doing this work	There is concern that secretaries will make mistakes in scheduling diagnoses that they are not familiar with	
	Gains from staying the same	**Losses from staying the same**	**Retain gains while eliminating losses**
No Change	Secretaries will continue to maintain the autonomy of structuring their day as they wish	Secretaries will contine to avoid working referrals because the process is cumbersome and confusing	Have secretaries work with providers in their subspecialities to help create the reference materials for all secretaries
	Secretaries with subspeciality knowledge will be scheduling their own referrals	Patients will continue to wait upwards of 4-6 weeks to schedule their appointment	Have flexibility in the hours that secretaries spend working on referrals - secretaries are scheduled to focus on referrals for four hours on their day of the week, but they can do this whenever it makes sense around their other tasks that day

Another option for assessing the environment is to consider all of the forces working toward and against the proposed change. A good tool for this is the force field analysis as it also allows you to assign weight to each force and determine if you have more forces working towards or against the change.

Tool: Force Field Analysis

PURPOSE: To understand both the helping and the hindering forces toward a proposed change to assess if there are more forces for or against the change.

HOW TO COMPLETE:

1. Enter the proposed change into the center lane of the template.

2. Brainstorm a list of helping and hindering forces for the proposed change and enter them into two columns, on either side of the change.

3. Look at each helping and hindering force individually and determine the proper weight of that force (high, medium, or low). A high force is one with a large impact, a low force is one with little impact. Total the counts to get a sense of which forces are stronger – those helping or those hindering your work.

4. Once the team is done listing and weighing individual forces, use the chart to start planning strategies to capitalize on the helping forces and mitigate the hindering forces. Focus on those that are most highly weighted first.

Tips:

- Once the team has brainstormed both help-ing and hindering forces, it can be helpful to look at each list one more time and see if the opposite of any statements are true. Sometimes a helping force might be related to a similar hindering force.

- We use high, medium, low as the rating fields. Your team can create a different scale if there is another rating system that would help differ-entiate between factors better (i.e. 1-5 ratings). Be sure to keep any rating system consistent throughout all of the factors.

Example:
Delirium Bundle Implementation

In the force field analysis example below, a team working in the ICU to implement a delirium reduction bundle to help reduce the incidence and duration of delirium in the patient population had a team discussion on helping and hindering forces for the change. The team had good stakeholder representation and an open and honest dialogue about some of the barriers and challenges they anticipate facing for the change.

Forces For Change	Weight		Change Proposal		Forces Against Change	Weight
Engaged team	H				Hard to see the benefit in your shift	M
Past performance motivates	M				Burden of another screening tool - more documentation	H
Many interested staff members	H		Implement Delirium Bundle in the ICU		A lot of stakeholders, hard to keep everyone on the same page	H
Decrease LOS, financial and access impact	H				Clarity of ownership of delirium management	H
Decrease sentinel events	M				Major change in staff/provider clinical practice	H
Recent literature	M				Stress level of staff - resource support	M
Patient and family centric focus	M				Nursing turnover rate	M

		Count of Weight Totals			
	H - High	3		4	H - High
	M - Medium	4	Weight	3	M - Medium
	L - Low	0		0	L - Low

Finally, it can also be helpful to consider assessing the people involved in the change. We're not talking a psychometric personalty assessment (let's save that for another book), we mean assessing the relationships between the people and the influence that they have on each other. Having an understanding of how people work together can help you to leverage relationships during a change or warn you of potential barriers to implementing something new.

Tool: Influence Map

PURPOSE: To visually describe the degree of influence individual stakeholders have on the project and the amount of influence between project stakeholders.

HOW TO COMPLETE:

1. Identify all of the stakeholders and other relevant individuals impacted by the project.

2. List each of the stakeholders in a circle.

3. Arrange the stakeholders and individuals in a large circle.

4. Start thinking about the relationships, partnerships, and conflicts among these stakeholders and individuals.

5. Using the appropriate connecter lines (see the legend), start to fill in lines that indicate the strength of the relationship and the type of relationship.

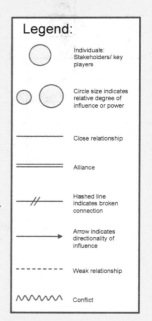

Legend:

◯ Individuals: Stakeholders/ key players

◯ ◯ Circle size indicates relative degree of influence or power

——— Close relationship

═══ Alliance

—//— Hashed line indicates broken connection

——→ Arrow indicates directionality of influence

- - - - Weak relationship

⋀⋀⋀⋀ Conflict

6. Use arrows to represent the direction of the influence.

7. Adjust the size of the circles to represent the strength of that individual's influence. The larger the circle, the larger the influence.

Tips:

- The influence map is particularly useful in understanding how stakeholder groups and individuals influence one another. This can help to identify ways to garner resources and support for project success.

- Many times this is utilized as a planning tool by you, the project leader, and perhaps completed working independently or with your sponsor.

- Once completed, the influence map can be used to help develop change management and communication tactics for your project.

- Be sure to focus on the current project when thinking about relationships. Sometimes workplace relationships can be very complex and vary depending on the topic or project. If this is the case for some stakeholders, draw the map in regard to the current project specifically.

Example:
Clinic Flow Project

An improvement leader was preparing to kick off an ambulatory clinic flow project in a specialty clinic. He completed an influence map based on his understanding of the key stakeholder relationships to help him plan communication and change management approaches for the project.

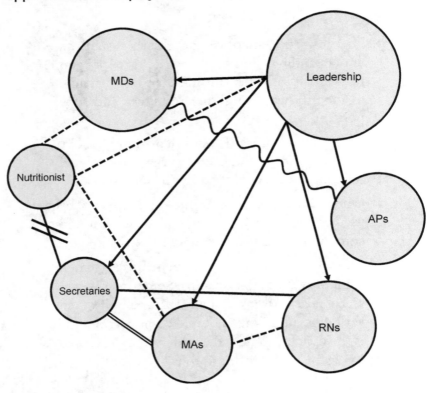

There you have it, your toolkit is officially complete! You will find no further tools in the remaining pages of this book. That being said, there are many other tools that people use in DMAIC project work, so if you ever feel like you need a tool for something that isn't listed in the book, go check out other resources. We have chosen to share with you the most common tools used in healthcare projects because we have seen many successful projects that have used selections from this toolkit.

In addition to tools, we have tried to share tips with you throughout the book. We want you to learn from the work we've done and the mistakes that we've made along the way. Not every project is going to go perfectly; even after doing dozens of projects, many of ours still do not go perfectly. We learn from each project and carry those lessons into our future work where those lessons might be relevant. Continuous improvement requires continuous learning, which means we have to be open to both success and failure. Never think of a bad project as a failure. We've had projects that started and stopped, projects that didn't implement the best possible solution, and projects that went well above what we thought possible at the outset. Each one was a success in its own way and an opportunity to learn and do something different the next time around. We wish you the best of luck on your future project work and your own journey to continuous improvement.

Acknowledgements

The contents of this book contain the creative fingerprints of so many amazing continuous improvement leaders from the Dartmouth-Hitchcock Health Community. Seriously, this book would not have been possible without the support of the individuals listed here.

Dr. George Blike championed establishing a standard set of methods and tools for building organizational capacity and competency in improvement for Dartmouth-Hitchcock Health. The foundational work to create the Value Institute Learning Center and kick-start the Lean Six Sigma training programs for the health system would not have happened without Dr. Sue McGrath's expertise and leadership. Thank you, George and Sue, for your vision and leadership – it is amazing to see what the Value Institute Learning Center has become today!

Thank you to the Value Institute Learning Center faculty – past, present, and future – for all of the time, effort and energy you have (and will continue to) put into making our Lean Six Sigma curriculum amazing for students. Your tips and tricks have made their way into this book to help set our readers up for success with utilizing the DMAIC toolkit. List of faculty past and present (including but not limited to): Victoria Adams, Joseph Caristi, Paul Christman, David Fittro, Erin Gooch, Daniel Herrick, Ryan LeFebvre, Dennis McGrath, Alison Mumford, Tomi Osunkoya, Victoria Patric, Otelah

ACKNOWLEDGEMENTS

Perry, Joel Preminger, Steve Sarette, Evelyn Schlosser, Sara Simeone, Chris Tkal, Aleksandra van Loggerenberg. We could go on about each of your individual contributions for pages, but we're going to save a tree. You have all left a mark on our curriculum and that is represented in this book.

Thank you to Meghan Boyer and Jennifer Cole for their support and coordination of our tools and templates in preparation for the development of this book. We also appreciate your rapid response to all pleas for IT assistance throughout the writing process! And thank you to Alyssa Lohmann for being the first set of eyes on the full book. Your feedback has been greatly appreciated and incorporated.

To our A+ storyboard student, Kathleen Stewart, thank you for allowing us to show off your work!

A big thank you to our graphics guru, Melissa Viens, for customizing our visual content to make it spiffy and easy for students to read and engage with.

Thank you to Sam Shields for your support of our crazy idea to turn the work we do on a daily basis into a book.

To the team members who participated on the real-life versions of the projects that we fictionalized, thank you for all your hard work. A special thank you to Dr. Carolyn Kerrigan who had a hand in both of the major example projects, as well as to all of the physician champions, data analysts, sponsors, and residents (that somehow managed to support this work despite their already crazy busy schedules).

Last, but not least, a big thank you to our students and the continuous improvement community at Dartmouth-Hitchcock Health. Your improvement efforts help support the pursuit of our vision to inspire sustainable improvement for every patient, every employee, every day.

About VILC

We are so thrilled that you are reading this book, and even more excited that you want to read the "About VILC" section. Seriously, how often do people read the acknowledgements and the "about" sections? It has to be a pretty good book for most people to bother. So, you're welcome for the fun and fancy-free journey through DMAIC that we have taken you on.

The Value Institute Learning Center is part of Dartmouth-Hitchcock Health. As you learned in Dr. Blike's foreword, we've been around since 2011 and have been teaching Yellowbelt and Greenbelt level Lean Six Sigma training since our inception. We have trained thousands of healthcare employees in our area on this methodology and every single one of our instructors loves this work and practices it daily. Our classes are available to anyone who is interested, even if you work in a different industry. All of our classes are taught through a healthcare lens, which makes them a great option for healthcare staff, but the concepts are transferable to just about any industry. If you are interested in learning more about the classes that we offer, you can peruse our website at **www.d-h.org/vilc** or email us at **VILearningCenter@hitchcock.org**. We love talking to people about Lean Six Sigma in healthcare (which is pretty impressive for a couple of introverts!). Feel free to reach out and ask us questions about how you can learn more or enroll in one of our classes. And, yes, we are this funny in person too!

About the Authors

DANIELLE M. POTTER, MS, LSSBB, PMP

Danielle started working in healthcare in 2011. As a clinically-diagnosable perfectionist, she started trying to improve just about every aspect of her work early on. As she pushed for better processes (and annoyed her coworkers), one (not annoyed) coworker contacted her about joining a Yellowbelt project team in 2013. From there, she was hooked. She attended both the Yellowbelt and Greenbelt trainings offered at the Value Institute, completed a Master's degree in Industrial and Organizational Psychology, completed her Lean Six Sigma Blackbelt certification and completed her Project Management Professionals Certification. Danielle currently works as an organizational development consultant and spent two years as Manager of the Value Institute Learning Center. She is also a Certified Instructional Designer and continues to work with peers on developing new trainings what will benefit healthcare workers. She is a true nerd at heart (you are welcome, fellow nerds, for the references in this book) and appreciates that her dog was willing to cuddle for most of the time that she spent writing this book. Her biggest regret is that Harry Potter references did not appear to relate to DMAIC.

NICOLE SZALAY BATULIS, MHA, LSSMBB, CPHQ

Nicole began her Lean Six Sigma learning journey by completing Greenbelt training during her post-graduate hospital administrative fellowship. Seeing the impact of applying her DMAIC skills in her first leadership role managing patient registration led her to seek out opportunities to lead improvement initiatives in healthcare full time. Nicole has a Bachelor's Degree in Chemistry and Violin Performance and a Master's in Healthcare Administration. Nicole has over 10 years of experience working in healthcare and has worked in academic medicine and teaching hospitals for her entire career. She achieved her Lean Six Sigma Master Blackbelt certification and is also a Certified Professional in Healthcare Quality. Nicole joined the performance improvement team at Dartmouth-Hitchcock in 2013 as a Senior Consultant and is currently the director of the Operational Excellence team. She is an East Coast transplant who grew up in tornado alley and is referred to by her teammates as "the calm in the storm." Nicole is passionate about making the Lean Six Sigma approach to problem solving accessible and relatable to all staff in the healthcare space, and that was what inspired the idea for this book.

Tools Index

If you're a page-flipper (and you've missed the awesomeness that was reading this book) – we've created an index just for you. Brush up on the instructions for a tool that you might be struggling with or one you're just curious to learn more about.

CPSIA information can be obtained
at www.ICGtesting.com
Printed in the USA
JSHW041944211220
10466JS00002B/2